Doing Sociology: A Global Perspective

Using MicroCase® ExplorIt

Fourth Edition

Rodney Stark
University of Washington

WADSWORTH
THOMSON LEARNING

Australia • Canada • Mexico • Singapore • Spain • United Kingdom • United States

Printed in Canada
1 2 3 4 5 6 7 05 04 03 02 01

0-534-58761-5

For more information about our products, contact us at:
Thomson Learning Academic Resource Center
1-800-423-0563

For permission to use material from this text, contact us by:
Phone: 1-800-730-2214
Fax: 1-800-731-2215
Web: www.thomsonrights.com

Asia
Thomson Learning
60 Albert Complex, #15-01
Albert Complex
Singapore 189969

Australia
Nelson Thomson Learning
102 Dodds Street
South Street
South Melbourne, Victoria 3205
Australia

Canada
Nelson Thomson Learning
1120 Birchmount Road
Toronto, Ontario M1K 5G4
Canada

Europe/Middle East/South Africa
Thomson Learning
Berkshire House
168-173 High Holborn
London WC1 V7AA
United Kingdom

Latin America
Thomson Learning
Seneca, 53
Colonia Polanco
11560 Mexico D.F.
Mexico

Spain
Paraninfo Thomson Learning
Calle/Magallanes, 25
28015 Madrid, Spain

CONTENTS

ABOUT THE AUTHOR

Rodney Stark grew up in Jamestown, North Dakota, and received his Ph.D. from the University of California, Berkeley, where he held appointments as a research sociologist at the Survey Research Center and the Center for the Study of Law and Society. He subsequently became Professor of Sociology and Comparative Religion at the University of Washington. Stark is the author of scores of scholarly articles and of twenty-two books—several of which have won national and international awards.

GETTING STARTED

INTRODUCTION

The goal of this workbook is to help you learn how to use data to explore the world of sociology and how to investigate new ideas and conduct research to test these ideas.

Each exercise in this workbook has two sections. The first section discusses a particular topic in sociology and demonstrates how data are used to support, augment, and test the ideas proposed. It is possible to read this section without using your computer. However, all of the graphics in the text can be created on your computer by following the ExplorIt Guide, which is described below. Ask your instructor whether you should follow along the first section of each exercise with a computer.

The worksheet section allows you to follow up on these ideas by doing your own research. You will use the student version of ExplorIt to complete these worksheets.

SYSTEM REQUIREMENTS

- Windows 95 (or higher)

- 8 MB RAM

- CD-ROM drive

- 3.5" disk drive

- 15 MB of hard drive space (if you want to install it)

NETWORK VERSIONS OF STUDENT EXPLORIT

A network version of Student ExplorIt is available at no charge to instructors who adopt this book for their course. It's worth noting that Student ExplorIt can be run directly from the CD and diskette on virtually any computer network—regardless of whether a network version of Student ExplorIt has been installed.

INSTALLING STUDENT EXPLORIT

If you will be running Student ExplorIt directly from the CD-ROM and diskette—or if you will be using a version of Student ExplorIt that is installed on a network—skip to the section "Starting Student ExplorIt."

To install Student ExplorIt to a hard drive, you will need the diskette and CD-ROM that are packaged inside the back cover of this book. Then follow these steps in order:

1. Start your computer and wait until the Windows desktop is showing on your screen.

2. Insert the diskette into the A drive (or B drive) of your computer.

3. Insert the CD-ROM disc into the CD-ROM drive of your computer.

4. On most computers the CD-ROM will automatically start and a welcome menu will appear. If the CD-ROM doesn't automatically start, do the following:

   Click [Start] from the Windows desktop, click [Run], type **D:\SETUP**, and click [OK]. (If your CD-ROM drive is not the D drive, replace the letter D with the proper drive letter.)

5. To install Student ExplorIt to your hard drive, select the second option on the list: "Install Student ExplorIt to your hard drive."

6. During the installation, you will be presented with several screens, as described below. In most cases you will be required to make a selection or entry and then click [Next] to continue.

The first screen that appears is the **License Name** screen. (If this software has been previously installed or used, it already contains the licensing information. In such a case, a screen confirming your name will appear instead.) Here you are asked to type your name. It is important to type your name correctly, since it cannot be changed after this point. Your name will appear on all printouts, so make sure you spell it completely and correctly! Then click [Next] to continue.

A **Welcome** screen now appears. This provides some introductory information and suggests that you shut down any other programs that may be running. Click [Next] to continue.

You are next presented with a **Software License Agreement**. Read this screen and click [Yes] if you accept the terms of the software license.

The next screen has you **Choose the Destination** for the program files. You are strongly advised to use the destination directory that is shown on the screen. Click [Next] to continue.

The Student ExplorIt program will now be installed. At the end of the installation, you will be asked if you would like a shortcut icon placed on the Windows desktop. It is recommended that you select [Yes]. You are now informed that the installation of Student ExplorIt is finished. Click the [Finish] button and you will be returned to the opening Welcome Screen. To exit completely, click the option "Exit Welcome Screen."

INSTALLING STUDENT EXPLORIT TO A LAPTOP COMPUTER

If you are installing Student ExplorIt to a hard drive on a laptop that has both a CD-ROM drive and a floppy disk drive, simply follow the preceding instructions. However, if you are installing Student ExplorIt to a hard drive on a laptop where you cannot have both the CD-ROM drive and floppy disk drive attached at the same time, follow these steps in order:

1. Attach the CD-ROM drive to your computer and insert the CD-ROM disc.

2. Start your computer and wait until the Windows desktop is showing on your screen.

3. On most computers the CD-ROM will automatically start and a welcome menu will appear. If it does, click Exit.

4. Click [Start] from the Windows desktop, select [Programs], and select [Windows Explorer].

5. Click the drive letter for your CD-ROM in the left column (usually D:\). A list of folders and files on the CD-ROM will appear in the left column.

6. From the Windows Explorer menu, click [Edit] and [Select All]. The folders and files on the CD-ROM will be highlighted. Using your mouse, right click (use your right mouse button) on the list of folders and files. From the box that appears select [Copy].

7. In the left column of the Windows Explorer menu, right click once on your C drive (do NOT select a folder) and select [Paste] from the box that appears.

8. Close Windows Explorer by clicking the [X] button on the top right corner.

9. Remove the CD-ROM and CD-ROM drive from your computer and attach the floppy disk drive. Place the floppy disk drive from your workbook in the drive.

10. Click [Start] from the Windows desktop, click [Run], type C:\SETUP and click [OK].

11. Select the first option from the Welcome menu: **Run Student ExplorIt from the CD-ROM**. Within a few seconds Student ExplorIt will appear on your screen.

STARTING STUDENT EXPLORIT

There are three ways to run Student ExplorIt: (1) directly from the CD-ROM and diskette, (2) from a hard drive installation, or (3) from a network installation. Each method is described below.

Starting Student ExplorIt from the CD-ROM and Diskette

Unlike most Windows programs, it is possible to run Student ExplorIt directly from the CD-ROM and diskette. To do so, follow these steps:

1. Insert the 3.5" diskette into the A or B drive of your computer.

2. Insert the CD-ROM disc into the CD-ROM drive.

3. On most computers the CD-ROM will automatically start and a welcome menu will appear. (Note: If the CD-ROM does **not** automatically start after it is inserted, click [Start] from the Windows desktop, click [Run], type D:\SETUP and click [OK]. If your CD-ROM drive is not the D drive, replace the letter D with the proper drive letter.)

4. Select the first option from the Welcome menu: **Run Student ExplorIt from the CD-ROM**. Within a few seconds Student ExplorIt will appear on your screen.

Starting Student ExplorIt from a Hard Drive Installation

If Student ExplorIt is installed to the hard drive of your computer (see earlier section "Installing Student ExplorIt"), it is **not** necessary to insert either the CD-ROM or floppy diskette. Instead, locate the Student ExplorIt "shortcut" icon on the Windows desktop, which looks something like this:

To start Student ExplorIt, position your mouse pointer over the shortcut icon and double-click (that is, click it twice in rapid succession). If you did not permit the shortcut icon to be placed on the desktop during the install process (or if the icon was accidentally deleted), you can alternatively follow these directions to start the software:

Click [Start] from the Windows desktop.

Click [Programs].

Click MicroCase.

Click Student ExplorIt.

After a few seconds, Student ExplorIt will appear on your screen.

Starting Student ExplorIt from a Network

If the network version of Student ExplorIt has been installed to a computer network, you must insert the floppy diskette (not the CD-ROM) that comes with your book. Then double-click the Student ExplorIt icon that appears on the Windows desktop to start the program. (Note: Your instructor may provide additional information that is unique to your computer network.)

MAIN MENU OF STUDENT EXPLORIT

Student ExplorIt is extremely easy to use. All you do is point and click your way through the program. That is, use your mouse arrow to point at the selection you want, then click the left button on the mouse.

The main menu is the starting point for everything you will do in Student ExplorIt. Look at how it works. Notice that not all options on the menu are always available. You will know which options are available at any given time by looking at the colors of the options. For example, when you first start the software, only the OPEN FILE option is immediately available. As you can see, the colors for this option are brighter than those for the other tasks shown on the screen. Also, when you move your mouse pointer over this option, it is highlighted.

Step 1: Select a Data File

Before you can do anything in Student ExplorIt, you need to open a data file. To open a data file, click the OPEN FILE task. A list of data files will appear in a window (e.g., COUNTIES, GLOBAL, STATES, etc.). If you click on a file name *once*, a description of the highlighted file is shown in the window next to this list. To open the STATES file, click the [Open] button (or just double-click STATES). The next window that appears (labeled File Settings) provides additional information about the data file, including a file description, the number of cases in the file, and the number of variables, among other things. To continue, click the [OK] button. You are now returned to the main menu of Student ExplorIt. (You won't need to repeat this step until you want to open a different data file.) Notice that you can always see which data file is currently open by looking at the file name shown on the top line of the screen.

Step 2: Select a Task

Once you open a data file, the next step is to select a program task. Six analysis tasks are offered in this version of Student ExplorIt. Not all tasks are available for each data file, because some tasks are appropriate only for certain kinds of data. Mapping, for example, is a task that applies only to ecological data, and thus cannot be used with survey data files.

Click the MAPPING option with your left mouse button to select this task.

Step 3: Select a Variable

After a task is selected, you will be shown a list of the variables in the open data file. Notice that the first variable is highlighted and a description of that variable is shown in the Variable Description window at the lower right. You can move this highlight through the list of variables by using the up and down cursor keys (as well as the <Page Up> and <Page Down> keys). You can also click once on a variable name to move the highlight and update the variable description. Go ahead—move the highlight to a few other variables and read their descriptions.

If the variable you want to select is not showing in the variable window, click on the scroll bars located on the right side of the variable list window to move through the list. See the following figure:

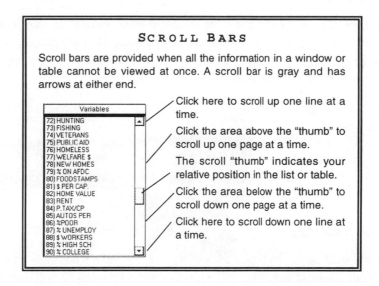

By the way, you will find an appendix at the back of this workbook that contains a list of the variable names for key data files provided in this package.

Each task requires the selection of one or more variables. Inside this box, there is a vertical cursor that indicates that this box is currently an active option. When you select a variable, it will be placed in this box. Before selecting a variable, be sure that the cursor is in the appropriate box. If it is not, place the cursor inside the appropriate box by clicking the box with your mouse. This is important because some situations will require more than one variable to be selected, and you want to be sure that you put each selected variable in the right place.

For this example, let's select variable 20) %DIVORCED. To select a variable, use any one of the methods shown below. (Note: If the name of a previously selected variable is in the box, use the <Delete> or <Backspace> key to remove it—or click the [Clear All] button.)

- Type the **number** of the variable and press <Enter>.

- Type the **name** of the variable and press <Enter>. Or you can type just enough of the name to distinguish it from other variables in the data—%DIV would be sufficient for this example.

- Double-click the desired variable in the variable list window. This selection will then appear in the variable selection box. (If the name of a previously selected variable is in the box, the newly selected variable will replace it.)

- Highlight the desired variable in the variable list, then click the arrow that appears to the left of the variable selection box. The variable you selected will now appear in the box. (If the name of a previously selected variable is in the box, the newly selected variable will replace it.)

Once you have selected your variable (or variables), click the [OK] button to continue to the final results screen.

Step 4: Select a View

The next screen that appears shows the final results of your analysis. In most cases, the screen that first appears matches the "view" indicated in the instructions. In this example, you are instructed to look at the Map view—that's what is currently showing on the screen. In some instances, however, you may need to make an additional selection to produce the desired screen.

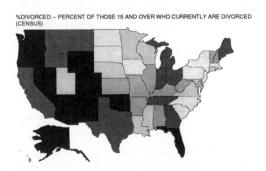

%DIVORCED -- PERCENT OF THOSE 15 AND OVER WHO CURRENTLY ARE DIVORCED (CENSUS)

(OPTIONAL) Step 5: Select an Additional Display

Some instructions will indicate that an additional "Display" should be selected. In that case, simply click on the option indicated for that additional display. For this example, select [Legend] to view the legend for the colors shown on the map.

Step 6: Continuing to the Next Variable

Some instructions may be the same for at least two examples in a row. For instance, after you display the map for divorce in the example above, you may be instructed to view a map for suicide using the same STATES data file and the same MAPPING task. With the results of your first analysis showing on the screen, there is no need to return to the main menu to complete this next analysis. Instead, all you need to do is select SUICIDE as your new variable. Click the [[↺]] button located in the top left corner of your screen and the variable selection screen for the MAPPING task appears again. Replace the variable with 22) SUICIDE and click [OK].

If you are instructed to select an entirely new task or data file, you will need to return to the main menu. To return to the main menu, simply click the [Menu] button located at the top left corner of the screen. At this point, select the new data file and/or task that is indicated in the instructions.

That's all there is to the basic operation of Student ExplorIt. Just follow the instructions and point and click your way through the program.

ON-LINE HELP

Student ExplorIt offers extensive on-line help. You can obtain task-specific help by pressing <F1> at any point in the program. For example, if you are performing a scatterplot analysis, you can press <F1> to see the help for the SCATTERPLOT task.

If you prefer to browse through a list of the available help topics, select **Help** from the pull-down menu at the top of the screen and select the **Help Topics** option. At this point, you will be provided a list of topic areas. Each topic is represented by a closed-book icon. To see what information is available in a given topic area, double-click on a book to "open" it. (For this version of the software, use only the "Student ExplorIt" section of help; do not use the "Student MicroCase" section.) When you double-click on a book graphic, a list of help topics is shown. A help topic is represented by a graphic with a piece of paper with a question mark on it. Double-click on a help topic to view it.

If you have questions about Student ExplorIt, try the on-line help described above. If you are not very familiar with software or computers, you may want to ask a classmate or your instructor for assistance.

EXITING FROM STUDENT EXPLORIT

If you are continuing to the next section of this workbook, it is *not* necessary to exit from Student ExplorIt quite yet. But when you are finished using the program, it is very important that you properly exit the software—do not just walk away from the computer or remove your diskette. To exit Student ExplorIt, return to the main menu and select the [Exit Program] button that appears on the screen.

Important: If you inserted your diskette and/or CD-ROM disc before starting Student ExplorIt, remember to remove it before leaving the computer.

EXERCISE 1:
SUICIDE AND SOCIAL FACTS

TASKS: Univariate, Cross-tabulation, Mapping
DATA FILES: SURVEY, STATES, GLOBAL

The English poet John Donne (1572–1631) expressed the fundamental truth on which sociology is based when he wrote that no human being "is an island." Every aspect of our humanity, from the language we speak to our hopes and dreams, is greatly determined by those around us. Consequently, it is impossible to study any human being as a completely isolated "island," which is why we use the term "social" science to refer to the many fields devoted to the study of human behavior: anthropology, criminology, economics, political science, psychology, social history, and sociology.

Of all social scientists, sociologists probably give the greatest emphasis to the social environment—to the group or collective aspects of human life. Put another way, the business of sociologists is to discover and explain what they call "social facts." The best way to understand what this fundamental term means is to retrace the process by which it came into use.

THE CONCEPT OF SUICIDE

Suicide has always caused a lot of concern. Why do some people take their own lives? Could they have been stopped? *Should* they have been stopped? Questions like that assume we agree on what we mean by the word "suicide." But, do we? Sometimes we say that a firefighter who tried to jump from a ladder into a burning building to save a child, took a "suicidal" risk. Is that the same kind of act as when someone about to be arrested for a brutal crime jumps off a cliff? Most people would say "no." Consequently, before we can study why people commit suicide, we need to agree on what we mean—we need a **concept** of suicide.

Concepts are names scientists use to identify some set or class of things as "alike." Biologists, for example, define all living organisms that give birth to live offspring, as opposed to laying eggs, as mammals. Used this way, *mammal* is a scientific concept that allows us to classify all living creatures as part of, or not part of, the set to be identified as mammals. Sociologists use many concepts. For example, a **group** is defined as any set of two or more persons who maintain a stable pattern of social relations over a period of time. Notice that this concept says nothing about the people making up the group. Just as the biological concept of mammal ignores all the many differences among cats, dogs, mice, and elephants (treating each as a member of the class of organisms defined as mammals), the concept of group ignores gender, race, age, and thousands of other traits of members, when identifying which sets of persons qualify as groups.

When the earliest sociologists began to study suicide, they defined it as consisting of actions taken for the primary purpose of ending one's life. Thus, the heroism of firefighters or soldiers is excluded because their own death was not their primary purpose, whereas jumping off a cliff in order to end one's life counts as suicide.

It is difficult to study persons who commit suicide, since we don't know who they are until they're dead. Some studies have been made of those who attempted suicide and failed. But survivors are, in many ways, quite different from those who succeeded, since they mainly used less certain methods (sleeping pills rather than firearms) and may have intended to survive—as indicated by the fact that they called someone and told them they were going to commit suicide. Other studies have attempted to reconstruct a portrait of individual suicides by examining records and interviewing friends and relatives of victims. Still other research on suicide involves asking living people about their attitudes concerning suicide. Of course, that assumes that people who think suicide is an acceptable act will be more likely to take their own lives.

OPEN FILE: SURVEY

This data file consists of two national samples interviewed in 1998 and 2000 as part of the General Social Surveys conducted by the National Opinion Research Center (NORC) at the University of Chicago. Each is a stratified random sample of the U.S. population age 18 and over. You will discover a lot more about survey studies, and especially these surveys, in Exercise 2. For now, it is enough to know that these two surveys have been merged into one, giving a total of 5,649 people who were interviewed.

You may now examine any variable that is included in this file by any of the methods explained in "Getting Started." By the way, a **variable** is anything that varies among the "things" being examined. In this instance, the "things" are individual American adults, and the variable is their attitude toward suicide.

On the menu select **Univariate**.

Enter the variable name or number: 19) SUICIDE?

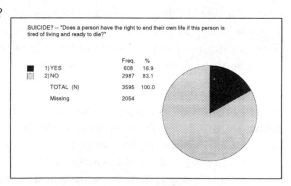

This graphic appears on your monitor screen. A random subsample of respondents were asked "Does a person have the right to end their own life if this person is tired of living and ready to die?" Of those asked, only 16.9 percent said "yes." Overwhelmingly, Americans reject the notion that people have the right to commit suicide (83.1 percent said "no"). Presumably, those who said "yes" would be more likely than those who said "no" to actually take their own lives, or to encourage or assist someone else in doing so.

Here we are examining these responses of individuals as if each was an "island." That is, the distribution of responses is based on 3,595 Americans of all sorts and from here and there across the nation. In some ways, the answer gives insight into the general American culture, but it leads to the obvious question: Do different kinds of Americans hold different views about suicide? Applied to humans, the idea that they come in various kinds is based on the fact that humans differ a lot in how others respond to them, in their life circumstances, as well as in their social surroundings.

On the menu screen select **Cross-tabulation**.

For the row variable select 19) SUICIDE?
For the column variable select 3) SEX.

CLICK ON: Column %

SUICIDE?   by   SEX
Cramer's V: 0.064 **

		SEX		
		MALE	FEMALE	TOTAL
SUICIDE?	YES	303	305	608
		19.7%	14.8%	16.9%
	NO	1235	1752	2987
		80.3%	85.2%	83.1%
	Missing	923	1131	2054
	TOTAL	1538	2057	3595
		100.0%	100.0%	

This table will appear on your screen. It compares men and women in terms of their approval of suicide. The data show that men are a bit more likely than women to approve of suicide. This is as it should be since men are, in fact, considerably more likely than women to attempt suicide and far more likely to succeed. For example, the current suicide rate for men is four times as high as the rate for women in both Canada and the United States. Now, let's compare people having different levels of education.

CROSS-TABULATION:
    Row Variable: 19) SUICIDE?
  Column Variable: 12) EDUCATION
        Column %

SUICIDE?   by   EDUCATION
Cramer's V: 0.142 **

		EDUCATION					
		NOT HSGRAD	HS GRAD	COLLEGE	GRAD SCHOL	Missing	TOTAL
SUICIDE?	YES	68	268	190	80	2	606
		12.6%	13.9%	22.5%	30.2%		16.9%
	NO	470	1664	654	185	14	2973
		87.4%	86.1%	77.5%	69.8%		83.1%
	Missing	331	1069	484	158	12	2054
	TOTAL	538	1932	844	265	28	3579
		100.0%	100.0%	100.0%	100.0%		

Here we see that the more education they have, the more likely people are to approve of suicide. Only 12.6 percent of those who did not finish high school approve, while 30.2 percent of those who went to graduate school approve.

CROSS-TABULATION:
    Row Variable: 19) SUICIDE?
    Column Variable: 17) PARTY PREF
        Column %

SUICIDE? by PARTY PREF
Cramer's V: 0.048 *

	PARTY PREF				
	DEMOCRAT	INDEPENDEN	REPUBLICAN	Missing	TOTAL
YES	294	121	166	27	581
	17.8%	17.6%	13.9%		16.5%
NO	1359	565	1024	39	2948
	82.2%	82.4%	86.1%		83.5%
Missing	909	357	722	66	2054
TOTAL	1653	686	1190	132	3529
	100.0%	100.0%	100.0%		

This table lets us compare people according to their political "group." Democrats and Independents are more likely to approve of suicide than are Republicans.

CROSS-TABULATION:
    Row Variable: 19) SUICIDE?
    Column Variable: 2) REGION
        Column %

SUICIDE? by REGION
Cramer's V: 0.114 **

	REGION				
	EAST	MIDWEST	SOUTH	WEST	TOTAL
YES	122	136	172	178	608
	16.9%	15.6%	13.3%	25.1%	16.9%
NO	602	734	1120	531	2987
	83.1%	84.4%	86.7%	74.9%	83.1%
Missing	413	496	735	410	2054
TOTAL	724	870	1292	709	3595
	100.0%	100.0%	100.0%	100.0%	

Finally, this table lets us compare different regions. The West stands out. People there are substantially more likely to approve of suicide than are people elsewhere, and approval is lowest in the South.

When faced with findings like this, sociologists often refer to them as "social facts." That is, they do not apply to individuals, but to collectivities. Although these tables are based on interviews with individuals, we don't really associate the fact that approval of suicide is highest in the western part of the nation with John who lives in Nevada or Joan who lives in Montana, but with Nevadans or Montanans.

OPEN FILE: STATES

Whenever we use the SURVEY data file, the "things" we examine are individuals, respondents who answered a specific set of questions. In this data set, the "things" we examine are the 50 American states. Of course, sociologists don't go around talking about the "things" they are examining. They call the things being compared the "units of analysis." So, in the SURVEY file the units of analysis are individuals. In this data file the units are states. When the units of analysis are geographic, they can be mapped as one method of comparison.

Doing Sociology

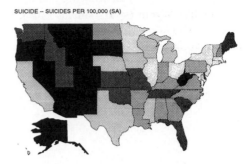

SUICIDE -- SUICIDES PER 100,000 (SA)

This map of the United States will appear on your screen. The 50 states are colored according to the level of their suicide rates—the annual number of suicides per 100,000 residents. Because these numbers are rates, they allow meaningful comparisons among units of different sizes. If we tried to compare the total number of suicides in each state, we would find that California is highest and Wyoming is lowest. But that's only because California has more than 30 million residents and Wyoming has fewer than 500,000. What we want to know is in which of these states people are more likely to commit suicide. Thus, we remove the differences in population size by, in effect, making every state the same size. As will be seen, when we do that we discover that people in Wyoming are far more likely to commit suicide than are people in California.

CLICK ON: Legend

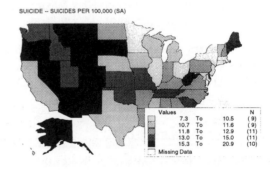

SUICIDE -- SUICIDES PER 100,000 (SA)

Values			N
7.3	To	10.5	(9)
10.7	To	11.6	(9)
11.8	To	12.9	(11)
13.0	To	15.0	(11)
15.3	To	20.9	(10)
Missing Data			

As shown, this legend will appear on your screen, displaying the range of suicide rates indicated by a given color. The principle employed is always the same: the darker the color, the higher the rate on any variable.

To remove the legend, **CLICK ON**: Legend.

Looking at the map, since the darker the state, the higher its rate, it is obvious that the states with the highest rates are clustered in the West. This confirms what we discovered above using individuals as units of analysis—people in the West were more likely to approve of suicide than were people else-where. There is a second way to compare states on this map.

CLICK ON: Spot Fill

Rather than depending only on different colors, here each state is *represented by a spot that is proportional* to the value of its suicide rate. The largest, darkest spots are mostly in the West.

Place the arrow on any nation shown on the map and **Click**.

The state will change color and the name of the state and its rate of suicides per 100,000 population will appear. Try Wyoming. Its suicide rate is 18.3 per 100,000. Now try California. Its rate is 10.7. You can move from state to state, examining each in this fashion. But, if you want to examine the entire list of states, ranked from highest to lowest:

CLICK ON: List: Rank

RANK	CASE NAME	VALUE
1	Nevada	20.9
2	Montana	19.8
2	Alaska	19.8
4	New Mexico	18.6
5	Wyoming	18.3
6	Colorado	18.2
7	South Dakota	16.9
8	Arizona	16.4
9	Oregon	16.2
10	West Virginia	15.3

Now you can see the actual suicide rate for all 50 states. Because not all 50 can fit on the screen at the same time, you may use the *page down key* or use the *mouse on the sidebar* to move along (the *page up key* lets you move back up the list as does the mouse).

At the top of the list is Nevada with 20.9 suicides per 100,000 population. Montana and Alaska are tied for second at 19.8. Then come New Mexico (18.6), Wyoming, and Colorado (18.2). California is in 40th place with a rate of 10.7, while New York and New Jersey are tied for last place with rates of 7.3.

Because states are *places*, not individuals, these data force us to think about suicide in *social* terms. When we do so, one thing is immediately obvious: Suicide is not mainly the result of the hustle, bustle, and stress of big-city life. These data might get us to thinking instead about loneliness and isolation as factors encouraging suicide.

OPEN FILE: GLOBAL

In this data file the units of analysis are nations. Like the states, nations differ a lot in terms of both area and the size of their populations. To create this set of 172 nations, all nations having populations of less than 200,000 were excluded.

MAPPING: 12) POPULATION

POPULATION -- TOTAL POPULATION IN MILLIONS (HDR)

Doing Sociology

This map shows nations according to their populations—the darker a nation, the larger its population.

CLICK ON: List: Rank

RANK	CASE NAME	VALUE
1	China	1255.7
2	India	1000.8
3	United States	288.0
4	Indonesia	206.3
5	Brazil	165.9
6	Pakistan	148.2
7	Russia	147.4
8	Japan	126.3
9	Bangladesh	124.8
10	Nigeria	106.4

Here we see the actual population for each nation in millions (add five zeros to get the full figures). China has the largest population at 1255.7 million, or more than 1 billion (1,244,700,000). India is second with just over a billion. The United States is third, followed by Indonesia and Brazil.

Western Samoa and Western Sahara have the smallest populations at 0.2 million, or about 200,000. A serious debate has been going on for some years as to whether Western Sahara is a nation or simply parts of Morocco and Mauritania. It was a Spanish protectorate until 1996. When the Spanish withdrew, Morocco annexed about half of the territory and Mauritania claimed the rest. However, those living there proclaimed their independence and have been conducting guerrilla warfare against outside forces. UN forces are now stationed there in an effort to keep the peace, and the UN has promised to hold an election to determine the future of the area—but the election has been postponed again and again.

MAPPING: 18) AREA

AREA -- AREA IN SQUARE MILES (SAUS)

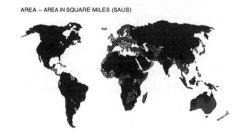

This map shows nations according to their areas (in square miles).

CLICK ON: List: Rank

RANK	CASE NAME	VALUE
1	Russia	6592817
2	China	3600930
3	Canada	3560219
4	United States	3539227
5	Brazil	3265061
6	Australia	2941285
7	India	1147950
8	Argentina	1056637
9	Kazakstan	1049150
10	Algeria	919591

Russia has the largest area: 6,592,817 square miles. China is second largest, closely followed by Canada, the United States, and Brazil. Malta (124) and Maldives (116) have the smallest areas. Malta is an island in the Mediterranean Sea and Maldives is an Island in the Indian Ocean.

MAPPING: 32) SUICIDE NO

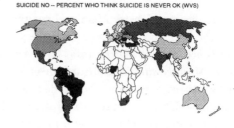

SUICIDE NO -- PERCENT WHO THINK SUICIDE IS NEVER OK (WVS)

Every five years or so, parallel survey studies are conducted in many nations—most of the same questions (translated into the local languages) are asked. These are referred to as the World Values Surveys (WVS), and the purpose of these studies is to allow for comparisons among nations. This map is based on a question asked of national samples of respondents in each of 61 nations: Is suicide ever justified? Respondents were asked to indicate their opinion on a ten-point scale from "never justified" to "always justified." The map shows the percentage in each of the nations who picked the lowest point on the scale: 1) never justified.

CLICK ON: List: Rank

RANK	CASE NAME	VALUE
1	Bangladesh	97
2	Brazil	87
3	Venezuela	83
4	Colombia	82
5	Macedonia	81
5	Turkey	81
7	Nigeria	78
8	Georgia	77
9	Moldova	76
10	Chile	73

The people of Bangladesh were the most opposed to suicide—97 percent said it is never justified. People in Brazil, Venezuela, and Colombia were next in their opposition. Nearly two-thirds of Americans said suicide is never justified. The bottom of the list is composed of European nations, with the Czech Republic (23 percent) nosing out Sweden (24 percent) for lowest in opposition to suicide.

You will notice that no value is given on this variable for the majority of the 172 nations. That is because no World Values Survey was conducted in these nations or, in several instances, this question on suicide was not included in the version of the WVS conducted there.

MAPPING: 51) SUICIDE

SUICIDE -- SUICIDES PER 100,000 (IP)

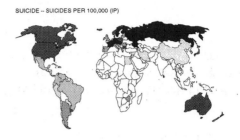

Here we see a map of suicide rates—the annual number of suicides per 100,000 population. Data are available for only 69 of the 172 nations. The map clearly shows that suicide rates are highest in Eastern Europe.

CLICK ON: List: Rank

RANK	CASE NAME	VALUE
1	Hungary	42.6
2	Sri Lanka	30.0
3	Finland	29.9
4	Denmark	26.6
5	Austria	23.1
6	Belgium	22.3
7	Switzerland	21.0
8	Russia	20.8
9	France	19.8
10	Luxembourg	18.6

Hungary has the highest suicide rate (42.6) closely followed by Sri Lanka (30.0). Canada's rate is 12.6 and the United States falls toward the middle with a rate of 11.7. Suicide rates are low in Latin America and in Islamic nations—Syria and Iran (0.2) have the lowest rates of all.

Now it's your turn.

NAME:

COURSE:

DATE:

REVIEW QUESTIONS

Based on the first part of this exercise, answer True or False to the following items:

A suicide rate is a social fact.	T F
The suicide rates for American states constitute a variable.	T F
In the SURVEY data set, suicide is the unit of analysis.	T F
New York has a very high suicide rate.	T F
Compared to Canada, the United States has a very high suicide rate.	T F

OPEN FILE: SURVEY

UNIVARIATE: 20) ABORT ANY?

1. What percentage of Americans agree that abortion ought to be legal for any woman who wants one, for any reason? _____%

2. What is the unit of analysis in the data file? _____

CROSS-TABULATION:
    ROW VARIABLE: 20) ABORT ANY?
  COLUMN VARIABLE: 3) SEX
          Column %

Copy the percentage who agree, as indicated.

	FEMALE	MALE
AGREE	_____%	_____%

3. It often is said that abortion is a woman's issue. Based on this table, how much difference would it make if only women were allowed to determine the legality of abortion?

_____

_____

_____

CROSS-TABULATION:
    ROW VARIABLE: 20) ABORT ANY?
  COLUMN VARIABLE: 12) EDUCATION
        Column %

Copy the percentage who agree, as indicated.

	NOT HS GRAD	HS GRAD	COLLEGE	GRAD SCHOOL
AGREE	_____%	_____%	_____%	_____%

4.   Which educational group is most supportive of abortion?   _____

5.   Which educational group is least supportive of abortion?   _____

6.   Can you suggest any reason for this difference?

    _____

    _____

    _____

    _____

    _____

CROSS-TABULATION:
    ROW VARIABLE: 20) ABORT ANY?
  COLUMN VARIABLE: 17) PARTY PREF
        Column %

Copy the percentage who agree, as indicated.

	DEMOCRAT	INDEPENDENT	REPUBLICAN
AGREE	_____%	_____%	_____%

7.   Which political group is most supportive of abortion?   _____

8.   Which political group is least supportive of abortion?   _____

9. Can you suggest any reason for this difference?

   _____

   _____

   _____

   _____

   _____

CROSS-TABULATION:
  ROW VARIABLE: 20) ABORT ANY?
COLUMN VARIABLE: 2) REGION
        Column %

Copy the percentage who agree, as indicated.

	EAST	MIDWEST	SOUTH	WEST
AGREE	_____%	_____%	_____%	_____%

10. In which region is there most support for abortion?   _____

11. In which region is there least support for abortion?   _____

   Looking back to the earlier results concerning suicide, how do the results for education, party preference, and region compare with those for abortion?

12. Education comparison:

13. Party preference comparison:

14. Regional comparison:

15. Do these comparisons suggest similarities (or differences) in attitudes toward suicide and abortion? Explain:

_____

_____

_____

_____

_____

OPEN FILE: STATES

MAPPING: 21) ABORTIONS

This map shows the number of abortions in each state per 1,000 women, aged 15 to 44.

16. How do the regional patterns shown on the map compare with those based on survey data? (circle one)   Similar   Different

17. Why do you suppose the rate is based on women rather than on the entire population?

_____

_____

_____

18. Why is the rate based only on women in this age group?

_____

_____

_____

CLICK ON: List: Rank

19. Which two states have the highest rank?   _____ and _____

20. Which two states have the lowest rank?   _____ and _____

21. What is the unit of analysis in this data file?   _____

OPEN FILE: GLOBAL

MAPPING: 22) ABORTION

This map shows the percentage of pregnancies terminated by abortion.

22. Some researchers think this is a better measure of the abortion rate than the one shown above for states. Can you suggest a reason why this measure might be better or worse?

_____

_____

_____

_____

23. Which five nations have the highest rates?   _____

_____

_____

_____

_____

24. Which three nations have the lowest rates?   _____

_____

_____

25. What is the unit of analysis in this data file?   _____

MAPPING: 24) AB. UNWANT

This map shows the percentage of respondents in 39 nations who approve of an abortion for a married woman who doesn't want another child.

26. Which nation is highest?   _____

27. Which nation is lowest?   _____

28. Does the United States more closely resemble the highest or the
lowest nation? (circle one)   Highest   Lowest

EXERCISE 2:
SEX AND SAMPLING

TASKS: Univariate, Cross-tabulation, Mapping
DATA FILES: SURVEY, GLOBAL, COUNTIES

OPEN FILE: SURVEY

Nearly every year since 1972, the National Opinion Research Center (NORC) at the University of Chicago conducts a survey (or public opinion poll) of a national sample of Americans 18 and over, known as the General Social Survey, or GSS. The people included in surveys often are referred to as the "respondents," because each person is asked to respond to a set of questions. Sometimes respondents are asked to fill out a questionnaire sent to them by mail, and sometimes an interviewer asks them each question and marks down the answer. The GSS uses interviewers.

What makes the GSS so valuable is that many questions are repeated every year and others are repeated every several years. This makes it possible to detect shifts in the answers people give over the years, and it also allows surveys from several years to be merged to create a larger number of cases, thus permitting study of somewhat smaller groups within the sample such as college students or widows.

This particular SURVEY data file was created by merging the 1998 and 2000 surveys (no survey was conducted in 1999 or in 2001). This gives a total of 5,649 Americans. However, some questions included in this data file were asked only in one of these years, while others were asked only of randomly selected subsamples within the larger survey.

Among the questions asked was "About how often did you have sex during the last 12 months?" Many people said "never." A few said "several times a day." To make the results easier to analyze, answers were translated into three large categories. Let's examine these.

UNIVARIATE: 23) SEX OFTEN?

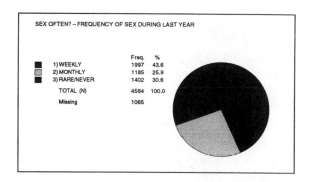

SEX OFTEN? -- FREQUENCY OF SEX DURING LAST YEAR

		Freq.	%
■	1) WEEKLY	1997	43.6
▩	2) MONTHLY	1185	25.9
■	3) RARE/NEVER	1402	30.6
	TOTAL (N)	4584	100.0
	Missing	1065	

About 4 persons out of 10 said they had sex at least once a week during the previous year. Another 25.9 percent said they had sex at least once a month. But nearly a third (30.6 percent) said they had very rarely or never had sex in the previous year. These statistics may come as a surprise to people who watch a lot of TV.

Another question asked was "Have you ever had sex with someone other than your husband or wife while you were married?" This question was not asked of people who had never been married. Judging from the mass media, it would seem that most—perhaps nearly all—Americans sooner or later cheat. Is that true?

UNIVARIATE: 21) UNFAITHFUL

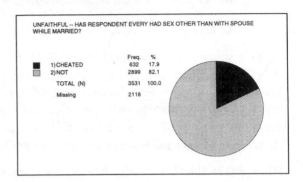

It appears that the media image is dead wrong: The overwhelming majority of Americans don't cheat. Only 17.9 percent said they had done so.

However, before we place too much confidence in these results, we must answer two obvious questions, both having to do with why we should believe poll results. First, will people answer honestly, or will lots of people lie in order not to have to tell an interviewer that, for example, they cheat on their spouse? Second, even if these particular people told the truth, how can we be sure they really represent all Americans?

One of the challenges of studying humans, as compared with atoms or ants, is that people are self-aware and they may try to fool anyone attempting to observe them or to find out what they do and what they really think. In many ways, social science is a game in which researchers try to figure out ways to keep from being fooled and people try to get around them. One very important thing researchers have learned is that people will be far more honest in answering an anonymous questionnaire than in confiding in an interviewer. Offsetting this are two facts: that questionnaires too often don't get sent back and that by using follow-up questions interviewers often can get far more accurate information. For example, when people are asked their occupation on a questionnaire, they too often just write vague answers such as "work at the bank" or "plumber." But an interviewer can probe: "What do you do at the bank?" and thus discover whether this person is the bank president or a teller. By probing the plumber's response, an interviewer can separate people who actually repair pipes from the owner of a large plumbing company. In addition, it is rather surprising how many people will tell interviewers about even sensitive topics—something the hosts of afternoon TV talk shows depend on. So, most of the time social scientists use interviewers when they can afford them—mail questionnaires are a lot cheaper.

In one important way, interviews and questionnaires are the same in that interviewers always work from a set of printed questions, reading each so that exactly the same wording is used with each respondent. This is extremely important. If this standard were not enforced, one interviewer might ask respondents: "Hey, you think it's okay to smoke marijuana, don't you?" And another interviewer might ask: "How do you feel about people using dangerous drugs like marijuana?" So, we don't let interviewers ask questions in their own words.

Sometimes, to gain the benefits of both methods, survey researchers use both an interviewer and a questionnaire, the latter being devoted to any sensitive topics such as sexual behavior. The interviewer asks all of the usual and nonthreatening questions and then gives the respondent a printed questionnaire and waits while the respondent fills it out and seals it in an envelope. That way the respondent doesn't forget to fill out the questionnaire or neglect to mail it back. And the interviewer never even sees the respondent's answers and anonymity is preserved. Later, a data entry clerk (often in an office several thousand miles away) unseals the envelope and adds these answers to the ones given to the interviewer. But this clerk never meets the respondent. A lot of effort has gone into evaluating this technique, and the results suggest that it yields quite accurate results—not perfect, but good enough.

OPEN FILE: GLOBAL

MAPPING: 31) INTERESTED

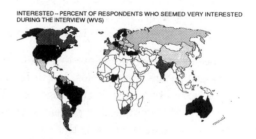

INTERESTED – PERCENT OF RESPONDENTS WHO SEEMED VERY INTERESTED
DURING THE INTERVIEW (WVS)

In each of the World Values Surveys, interviewers were asked to rate each respondent as to how interested they were during the interview. This map shows variations in the percent rated as "very interested."

CLICK ON: List: Rank

RANK	CASE NAME	VALUE
1	Turkey	80
2	Brazil	79
2	Netherlands	79
4	Colombia	77
5	United States	71
6	Germany	70
6	Nigeria	70
8	Sweden	68
10	Finland	67
10	Dominican Republic	67

Here we see that respondent's in Turkey were the most interested, followed by those in Brazil and then those in the Netherlands, Colombia, and the United States. In contrast, in some nations few respondents were very interested: China (27 percent), Ukraine (26 percent), Taiwan (23 percent) and Japan (20 percent). One must suppose that American surveys will be more accurate than surveys in Japan.

Now for the second major objection to surveys. How can it be that a few hundred, or even a few thousand, people can substitute for the whole nation? What makes us think that their answers represent everyone?

We accept the results from samples because of the laws of probability—the same ones that ensure that gambling casinos always come out ahead. When people are selected at random from a larger population, we can calculate the odds that persons included in the sample will be like those not included. That is, if we randomly select people from a population, as our sample grows in size it will come ever closer to matching the characteristics of the population from which it is selected. And the odds about how close it comes can be calculated and used to determine how confident we should be in the results.

You may have noticed that stories in the press based on surveys sometimes mention that the results are accurate within a particular percentage range—plus or minus 3 percentage points is a common range. For a sample of any given size, we can compute the probable range of accuracy of estimates based on the sample. With samples the size of this combined GSS, estimates of the actual distribution of answers to a given question should be accurate within about 2 percentage points, plus or minus. That is, if our results tell us that 17.3 percent say they have cheated on their spouse, 95 percent of the time the actual percentage in the population will be somewhere between 15.3 and 19.3 percent. This range is referred to as the **confidence interval**.

Let's see a concrete example. Since these data are from two separate national samples, we can examine differences across the two samples. Any differences must be due almost entirely to random fluctuation (things like sexual behavior don't change very fast). And, in fact, there are small differences from year to year. In the 1998 sample, 29.8 percent said they had rarely or never had sex in the past year; in the 2000 sample, 31.4 percent gave this answer. Each of the sample percentages is very close to the average for the two samples (30.6 percent). These small differences are due to random variation, but each result remains within the confidence interval. The actual percentage for the entire population remains unknown, but we can be very sure that it is within a percentage point or two of the average of the two years. And that's close enough.

But, random fluctuations and respondent truthfulness are not the only sources of errors in surveys. Bias arises to the extent that people selected as respondents refuse to take part.

OPEN FILE: SURVEY

UNIVARIATE: 3) SEX

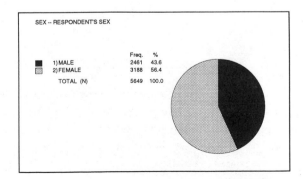

SEX -- RESPONDENT'S SEX

		Freq.	%
■	1) MALE	2461	43.6
▨	2) FEMALE	3188	56.4
	TOTAL (N)	5649	100.0

Doing Sociology

Here we see the sample broken down by gender. It shows that 56.4 percent are women and 43.6 percent are men. But, in the actual American population over age 18, women make up only 51.6 percent. All surveys are biased in terms of gender to about this extent for three reasons. First, those serving in the military and institutionalized populations (such as those in prison or jail) are not included in surveys. These populations are overwhelmingly male. Second, the population lacking a permanent address, such as homeless people and those staying with others (often with a woman who has an address), also are mostly men. Finally, men are more likely than women to refuse to be interviewed. Hence, behaviors and attitudes associated with gender will be somewhat inaccurate in most surveys because there are more female respondents than there should be. When it matters a lot, surveys correct for this shortage of men by adding a weight to increase the impact of the male respondents.

There is a final matter in trusting surveys that has to do with how the actual sample is drawn. If we could just put every Americans' name on a slip in a huge barrel, whirl the barrel, and then select names, we would have an entirely random sample and it would be accurate within the range of random fluctuation. But there is no complete list of American names and we can't select our sample that way. Furthermore, surveys are conducted by interviewers and so the respondents assigned to a given interviewer must be within easy traveling distance from her or his home. That wouldn't be necessary if the interviews were done by telephone, as many surveys are, but the results of phone surveys are extremely biased. For one thing, nearly everyone with answering machines or voice mail is missed. As a result, higher income people are very undersampled. Therefore, good survey studies such as the GSS use face-to-face interviews, and respondents are selected in two stages. First, a number of "sampling points" are selected across the nation. The General Social Surveys are based on 100 sampling points as shown in the map. Then individuals to be interviewed are randomly selected in the immediate vicinity of each sampling point.

Map of United States showing each NORC PSU

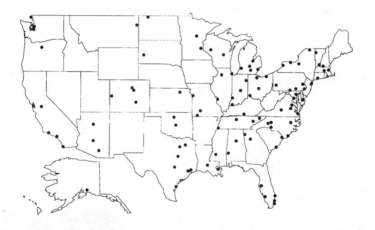

This technique, which is called **stratified**, **random sampling**, is accurate so long as any given trait is distributed randomly geographically. But, for traits that are very clustered in some places and not others, this technique will tend to over- or underrepresent such traits. Looking carefully at the map, you will notice that there is no sampling point in Utah. That means that Mormons will be undersampled. Since there also is no sampling point in Wyoming, that may cause cowboys and ranchers to be undersampled.

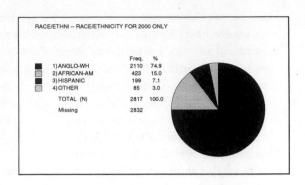

RACE/ETHNI -- RACE/ETHNICITY FOR 2000 ONLY

		Freq.	%
■	1) ANGLO-WH	2110	74.9
	2) AFRICAN-AM	423	15.0
■	3) HISPANIC	199	7.1
	4) OTHER	85	3.0
	TOTAL (N)	2817	100.0
	Missing	2832	

Here we see the racial and ethnic composition of the 2000 survey (until that year, people were not asked whether they were Hispanic). The percentages in the GSS Survey are not entirely correct. According to the Census of 2000, here's what they ought to be:

Non-Hispanic Whites	68.3%
African Americans	12.2%
Hispanic	12.1%
Other	7.4%

Asian	4.0
American Indian	1.2
Pacific Islander	0.2
Mixed Ancestry	1.9

TOTAL	100.0

These discrepancies are due to the fact that race and ethnicity are very concentrated geographically. Let's see.

OPEN FILE: COUNTIES

MAPPING: 11) % HISPANIC

% HISPANIC -- % HISPANIC (CENSUS)

This is a map of the 3,141 American counties showing the percent Hispanic in each according to the 2000 Census. (Hawaii and Alaska are not shown on the map, but their counties are included in the calculations.) Notice how greatly concentrated Hispanics are in the Southwest, precisely where there are relatively few sampling points. And that's mainly why they are so underrepresented in the survey.

MAPPING: 9) % ASIAN

% ASIAN -- % ASIAN (CENSUS)

Here is the county map for the Asian population. Asians are concentrated on the West Coast, and especially in Hawaii (not shown) where more than 40 percent of the population is of Asian ancestry (if you click on: list rank, the top counties all are in Hawaii). But, as you can see on the map of sampling points, there are none in Hawaii. And that's one reason why the "Other" group is too small in the sample. Another reason is that American Indians are very undersampled because they are concentrated in western states having no, or few, sampling points.

For these reasons the univariate distributions on any specific question may be inaccurate to the degree that answers differ across racial and ethnic groups. When it is important that these distributions be highly accurate (as when trying to predict an election), the results are weighted to bring racial and ethnic groups to their precise levels in the population. For example, if a group has only half as many respondents as it should have, we can double their responses when we calculate the overall distribution of answers.

So, now that you have some notion of why and how samples work, let's explore American sexual activity in a somewhat more specific way.

OPEN FILE: SURVEY

CROSS-TABULATION:
    Row Variable: 23) SEX OFTEN?
    Column Variable: 9) MARRYSINGL
    Column %

SEX OFTEN?   by   MARRYSINGL
Cramer's V: 0.258 **

		MARRYSINGL			
		MARRIED	SINGLE	Missing	TOTAL
SEX OFTEN?	WEEKLY	1158	481	358	1639
		54.1%	42.2%		50.0%
	MONTHLY	703	262	220	965
		32.9%	23.0%		29.4%
	RARE/NEVER	278	398	726	676
		13.0%	34.9%		20.6%
	Missing	485	234	346	1065
	TOTAL	2139	1141	1650	3280
		100.0%	100.0%		

alwaysuse colomn %

Row Variable isalways Dependant

the colomn is independant

Exercise 2: Sex and Sampling

23

Here we can see that more than half (54.1 percent) of married people had sex at least once a week or more often during the previous year, but a smaller percentage (42.2 percent) of the unmarried had sex this frequently. In contrast, reading across the bottom row of the table, we see that more than a third (34.9 percent) of unmarried people rarely or never had sex while only 13 percent of married people had sex that seldom.

However, before we accept these findings, there is one additional issue to confront.

As noted, random sampling is the basis of all survey research. Rather than interview all members of a population, survey researchers interview only a sample. As long as this sample is selected randomly, so that all members have an equal chance of being selected, the results based on the sample can be generalized to the entire population. That is, the laws of probability allow us to **calculate the odds** that something observed in the sample accurately reflects a feature of the population sampled—subject to **two limitations**.

First of all, the sample must be sufficiently **large**. Good survey studies are based on 1,000 cases or more. The larger the better: this merged sample includes 5,649 respondents.

The second limitation has to do with the **magnitude** (or size) **of the difference or relationship** observed. Because samples are based on the principle of random selection, they are subject to some degree of random fluctuation. That is, for purely random reasons there can be small differences between the sample and the population. Thus, whenever we examine cross-tabulations such as the one shown above, social scientists always must ask whether they are seeing a real difference, one that would turn up if the entire population were examined, or only a random fluctuation which does not reflect a true difference in the population.

Fortunately, there is a simple technique for calculating the odds that a given difference is real or random. This calculation is called a **test of statistical significance**, and differences observed in samples are said to be statistically significant when the *odds against* random results are high enough. There is no mathematical way to determine just how high is high enough. But through the years social scientists have settled on the rule of thumb that they will ignore all differences unless the odds are at least 20 to 1 against their being random. Put another way, social scientists reject all findings when the probability they are not random is greater than 5 in 100. What this level of significance means is that if 100 random samples were drawn independently from the same population, a difference this large would not turn up more than 5 times, purely by chance. In fact, many social scientists think this is too lenient a standard, and some even require that the probability that a finding is random be less than .01, or 1 in 100. Really big differences will result in odds greater than 1,000 to 1 that the result is not random. To apply these rules of thumb, social scientists calculate the **level of significance** of the differences in question and compare them against these standards.

If you look at the upper left of the screen showing the table shown above, you will read Cramer's V = 0.266**. For now, ignore everything except the two asterisks. One asterisk means that the odds are better than 20 to 1 that observed differences are real rather than merely random. Two asterisks means the odds are better than 100 to 1 that the observed differences are real. When there are no asterisks, that means the differences are *not* statistically significant. You should treat all tables without asterisks as if there were no differences. In this instance, if there were no asterisks following the value of V, we would be forced to conclude that our hypothesis was rejected and that married people were not significantly more likely than single people to have sex. But that's not what we found. The two asterisks tell us that married people are significantly more likely than single people to report having weekly sex.

Number of Asterisks	Conclusion
None	Not significant, ignore the differences
One	Significant differences (odds greater than 20 to 1)
Two	Significant differences (odds greater than 100 to 1)

Let's do another cross-tabulation. Proceed exactly as above, only this time change the column variable to 2) REGION.

CROSS-TABULATION:
Row Variable: 23) SEX OFTEN?
Column Variable: 2) REGION
Column %

SEX OFTEN?   by   REGION
Cramer's V: 0.034

		REGION				
		EAST	MIDWEST	SOUTH	WEST	TOTAL
SEX OFTEN?	WEEKLY	368	524	698	407	1997
		41.8%	45.4%	43.0%	43.9%	43.6%
	MONTHLY	218	271	442	254	1185
		24.8%	23.5%	27.3%	27.4%	25.9%
	RARE/NEVER	294	360	482	266	1402
		33.4%	31.2%	29.7%	28.7%	30.6%
	Missing	257	211	405	192	1065
	TOTAL	880	1155	1622	927	4584
		100.0%	100.0%	100.0%	100.0%	

Here we have separated everyone in the data file according to the region in which they live. Comparing across the table we can see that the East differs from the other three regions—people living in the East are more likely to report infrequent sex (33.4 percent) and less likely to report weekly sex (41.8 percent).

However, before you call the news media to tell them of this strange finding, notice Cramer's V: 0.034. There are no asterisks. The odds against this being a random finding are less than 1 in 20. *Treat this result as zero!*

THE HYPOTHESIS

Social scientists don't usually just pick their variables out of a hat. Usually, they have specific reasons to examine any particular cross-tabulation. That is, they begin with a definite expectation about what they are going to find. Sometimes such an expectation will be no more than a hunch or a suspicion. Often it is far more definite, being based on a theory, on experience, or even just on common sense—as in the case of expecting married people to have sex more often. But whatever its source, expectations about what will be found usually determine what variables to examine and are stated *before* any data are examined. When this is the case, scientists refer to their expectation or prediction as a hypothesis. So let's propose, and then test, some hypotheses about happiness.

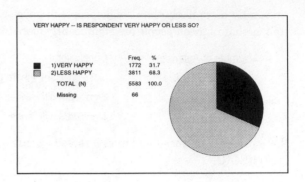

Respondents were asked if they were very happy or less happy. Nearly a third (31.7 percent) of Americans said they were very happy.

Hypothesis: *Men are more likely than women to say they are very happy.* Now we know what has been predicted, or hypothesized. Let's see if the data agree.

CROSS-TABULATION:
    Row Variable: 29) VERY HAPPY
    Column Variable: 3) SEX
        Column %

VERY HAPPY   by   SEX
Cramer's V: 0.015

		SEX		
		MALE	FEMALE	TOTAL
V E R Y H A P P Y	VERY HAPPY	752	1020	1772
		30.9%	32.4%	31.7%
	LESS HAPPY	1680	2131	3811
		69.1%	67.6%	68.3%
	Missing	29	37	66
	TOTAL	2432	3151	5583
		100.0%	100.0%	

Reading across the table from left to right, we can see that men (30.9 percent) are slightly less likely than women (32.4 percent) to say they are very happy. This forces us to reject the hypothesis since it predicted that men would be happier. Moreover, there are no asterisks by the value of V. Therefore we must treat the difference between men and women as zero. That too, of course, forces us to reject the hypothesis since we predicted a significant difference in favor of men.

Let's try another.

Hypothesis: *Younger people are more likely than older people to say they are very happy.* Now we know what has been predicted, or hypothesized. Again, let's see if the data agree.

CROSS-TABULATION:
    Row Variable: 29) VERY HAPPY
    Column Variable: 7) OVR/UND 50
        Column %

VERY HAPPY   by   OVR/UND 50
Cramer's V: 0.055 **

		OVR/UND 50			
		UNDER 50	50 & OVER	Missing	TOTAL
V E R Y H A P P Y	VERY HAPPY	1052	718	2	1770
		29.8%	35.1%		31.8%
	LESS HAPPY	2476	1326	9	3802
		70.2%	64.9%		68.2%
	Missing	46	19	1	66
	TOTAL	3528	2044	12	5572
		100.0%	100.0%		

Wrong again! Older people are more likely to be very happy. Two asterisks tell us that the difference is highly significant. The hypothesis must be rejected.

Hypothesis: *People with higher incomes are more likely than people with less income to say they are very happy.* Again, let's see if the data agree.

CROSS-TABULATION:
    Row Variable: 29) VERY HAPPY
    Column Variable: 11) $ –50/+50K
        Column %

VERY HAPPY   by $ -50/+50K
Cramer's V: 0.153 **

		$ -50/+50K			
		UNDER $50K	$50K & MOR	Missing	TOTAL
V E R Y H A P P Y	VERY HAPPY	070	825	77	1605
		26.3%	40.9%		31.8%
	LESS HAPPY	2439	1190	182	3629
		73.7%	59.1%		68.2%
	Missing	41	19	6	66
	TOTAL	3309	2015	265	5324
		100.0%	100.0%		

Correct! People having family incomes of $50,000 or more are substantially more likely to say they are very happy. Two asterisks mean this finding is highly significant.

Your turn.

EXERCISE 3:
COMPARISONS AND CORRELATIONS

TASKS: Mapping, Scatterplot
DATA FILES: GLOBAL, STATES

The map below ranks nations in terms of per capita (per person) gross domestic product (GDP) per year in U.S. dollars. GDP measures the total value of all goods and services produced within a nation during any given year. Economists regard GDP per capita as the best measure available for comparing countries in terms of their affluence or poverty.

OPEN FILE: GLOBAL

MAPPING: 3) $ GDP/CAP

$ GDP/CAP -- GROSS DOMESTIC PRODUCT PER CAPITA IN $US (HDR)

The map shows very clearly that, on a global scale, wealth and poverty are extremely regional. This is even clearer with a spot map.

Click on: Spot Fill.

$ GDP/CAP -- GROSS DOMESTIC PRODUCT PER CAPITA IN $US (HDR)

The large, dark spots are heavily concentrated in Europe, and others identify Canada, the United States, Japan, Australia, New Zealand, and the oil-rich nations along the Persian Gulf. In contrast, the tiny dots cluster in Africa, especially south of the Sahara, and in Asia, with some located in Latin America.

LIST RANK

RANK	CASE NAME	VALUE
1	Luxembourg	33505
2	United States	29605
3	Norway	26342
4	Switzerland	25512
5	Kuwait	25314
6	Iceland	25110
7	Denmark	24218
8	Singapore	24210
9	Canada	23582
10	Japan	23257

Tiny Luxembourg, a nation of international banks, has the highest per capita GDP ($33,505) followed by the United States ($29,605), Norway, Switzerland, and Kuwait. Tanzania ($480) and Sierra Leone ($458) have the lowest GDP per capita. To put these numbers in perspective, for every dollar of GDP produced in Sierra Leone, Americans produce (and enjoy) more than $64.

Now, let's do something different.

COMPARING MAPS:
    Variable 1: 3) $ GDP/CAP
    Variable 2: 26) CARS/1000

$ GDP/CAP -- GROSS DOMESTIC PRODUCT PER CAPITA IN $US (HDR)

CARS/1000 -- NUMBER OF AUTOMOBILES PER 1000 POPULATION (WA)

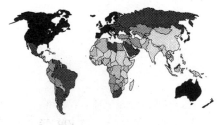

In the previous exercise, you were introduced to the term *hypothesis* and examined a number of cross-tabulations to see if they supported or rejected a hypothesis. Social scientists compare maps for the same reason that they look at cross-tabulations—to test hypotheses. Moreover, most hypotheses at least imply, and often state, a cause-and-effect relationship. For example, the hypothesis that people with higher incomes will be more likely to say they are very happy doesn't just assert that as if it were some kind of coincidence. That hypothesis implies a causal relationship—that income *causes* happiness.

What do we mean when we say that something is the cause of something else? We are saying that something makes something else happen. A **cause** is anything producing a result, an effect, or a consequence. Put another way, in causal relationships, variations in one variable cause variations in another variable. And to determine whether a causal relationship exists between two variables, the first test to be met is to show that one varies in tandem with the other—that people's happiness is higher or lower as their income is higher or lower.

It will be helpful to distinguish between **independent** and **dependent** variables. If we think something might be the cause of something else, we say that the *cause is the independent variable* and that the *consequence* (or the thing that is being caused) *is the dependent variable*. To help you remember the difference, think that variables being caused are dependent on the causal variable, whereas causal variables are not dependent, but are independent. In the example above, happiness is the dependent variable and income is the independent variable.

A primary reason to compare maps is to see if something might be causing something else. In this instance, GDP per capita is the independent variable which we suspect is causing how many people in a nation can afford a car.

Obviously these maps look a lot alike and therefore suggest that there may be a causal relationship between GDP and cars per 1,000 population. Even so, it is not easy with the naked eye to tell just how much alike or unalike these two maps are.

Later in this exercise you will compare two maps of the United States based on the 50 states. You will find it much easier to say whether two of the maps based on states are very similar or very different than to compare maps like these based on 172 nations. It is even harder to compare maps based on the more than 3,000 U.S. counties. The more cases, or units, involved, the harder it is to compare maps simply by looking at them. Thus it was a considerable achievement when, in the 1890s, an Englishman by the name of Karl Pearson discovered an incredibly simple method for comparing maps or lists.

To see Pearson's method we can draw a horizontal line across the bottom of a piece of paper. We will let this line represent the map of per capita GDP. So, at the left end of this line we will write 458, which indicates Sierra Leone, the nation with the lowest GDP. At the right end of the line we will place the number 33505 to represent Luxembourg as the highest nation.

458   33505

Now we can draw a vertical line up the left side of the paper. This line will represent the map of car ownership. At the bottom of this line we will write 0.7 to represent Myanmar, the nation with proportionately the fewest cars. At the top we will write 546.4 to represent Italy, the nation with the most cars per 1,000.

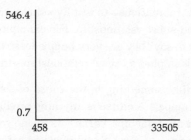

Now that we have a line with an appropriate scale to represent each map, the next thing we need to do is to refer to the distributions for each map in order to learn the value of each nation and then locate it on each line according to its score. Let's start with Luxembourg. Since it is the nation with the highest per capita gross domestic product, we can easily find its place on the horizontal line above. Make a small mark at 33505 to locate Luxembourg. Next, Luxembourg was second highest in terms of car ownership. So estimate where 540.0 is on the vertical line and make a mark there. Now, draw a line up from the mark for Luxembourg on the horizontal line and draw another out from the mark for Luxembourg on the vertical line. Where these two lines meet (or cross), draw a dot. This dot represents the *combined* map locations of Luxembourg. Next, let's locate the United States. To find the United States on the horizontal line, estimate where 29605 is located and make a mark at that spot. The U.S. is fourth on auto ownership, so locate 489.1 and mark that point on the vertical line. Now draw a line up from the mark on the horizontal line and draw one out from the mark on the vertical line. Where these two lines intersect is the combined map location for the United States.

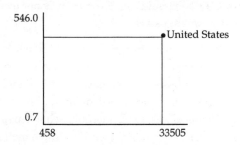

When we have followed this procedure for each nation, we will have 172 dots (minus those nations with missing data on either variable) located within the space defined by the vertical and horizontal lines representing the two maps. What we have done is to create a **scatterplot**. Fortunately, you don't have to go to all this trouble. *MicroCase ExplorIt* will do it for you.

SCATTERPLOT:
    Dependent Variable: 26) CARS/1000
    Independent Variable: 3) $ GDP/CAP

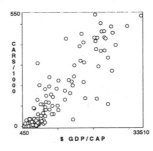

r = 0.901**   Prob. = 0.000   N = 159   Missing = 13

Each of these dots is a nation. *Use the mouse to put the arrow on a particular dot and click.* The name of this case appears at the left of the screen along with its value on each of the two variables. In addition, you are provided with information about what the correlation would be if you were to remove this case from the analysis.

Once Pearson had created a scatterplot, his next step was to calculate what he called the **regression line**. The regression line represents the best effort to draw a straight line that connects all of the dots. It is unnecessary for you to know how to calculate the location of the regression line—the program does it for you and it already is on the screen.

If you would like to see how the regression line would look if the maps were identical, all you need to do is examine the scatterplot for identical maps. So, if you create a scatterplot using CARS/1000 as both the dependent and independent variables, you will be comparing identical maps and the dots representing states will all be on the regression line like a string of beads.

However, since the maps for cars and for GDP per capita are only very similar, but not identical, most of the dots are scattered near, but not upon, the regression line. Pearson's method for calculating how much alike are any two maps or lists is very easy, once the regression line has been drawn. What it amounts to is measuring the distance out from the regression line to every dot.

CLICK ON: Residuals

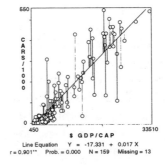

Line Equation   Y = -17.331 + 0.017 X
r = 0.901**   Prob. = 0.000   N = 159   Missing = 13

See all the little lines. If you added them all together, you would have a sum of the deviation of the dots from the regression line. The smaller this sum, the more alike are the two maps. For example, when the maps are identical and all the dots are on the regression line, the sum of the deviations is 0.

In order to make it simple to interpret results, Pearson invented a procedure to convert the sums into a number he called the **correlation coefficient**. The correlation coefficient varies from 0.0 to 1.0.

When maps are identical, the correlation coefficient will be 1.0. When they are completely unalike, the correlation coefficient will be 0.0. Thus, the closer the correlation coefficient is to 1.0 the more alike the two maps or lists. Pearson used the letter r as the symbol for his correlation coefficient.

Look at the lower left corner of the screen and you will see r = 0.901**. This indicates that the maps are extremely similar—that the two variables are highly correlated. To the right of the correlation coefficient you will see two asterisks. Just as with tables, this indicates statistical significance. In this case, the odds are more than 1 in 100 that this correlation is not the result of chance (recall the definitions of asterisks in Exercise 2). To the right of the level of significance is N = 159. In data analysis, N (often written as n) stands for the number of cases on which a calculation is based. In this instance we have data on both GDP and car ownership for 159 of the 172 nations. Finally, at the far right is Missing = 13. That tells us the data are missing for 13 cases (172 − 159 = 13).

Since Pearson invented r, many other correlation coefficients have been developed, each with special applications. Recall from the previous exercise that you were told to focus only on asterisks to determine whether or not the differences observed in a table are statistically significant. Thus, for example, the table cross-tabulating happiness and income produces this result: V = 0.172**. Now, it can be revealed: Cramer's V is a correlation coefficient designed for cross-tabulations. Like all correlation coefficients, V varies from 0.0 to 1.0, but for reasons that you need not learn in this course, correlations based on survey data (including V) produce smaller values than do those based on aggregate data. That is taken into account when significance is calculated, so continue to depend on the asterisks.

Correlation coefficients can be either *positive* or *negative*. The correlation between GDP and automobiles is positive. Where GDP is higher, so is car ownership. That is, as one rises so does the other—they tend to occur in unison. But when we examine a new scatterplot, the whole picture changes radically.

SCATTERPLOT:
   Dependent Variable: 15) FERTILITY
   Independent Variable: 16) CONTRACEP

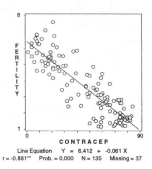

The dependent variable is the fertility rate, the number of children born to the average woman. The independent variable is the proportion of sexually active women in their childbearing years who are using contraceptives (or whose male partner is using some form of contraceptive). Where contraceptive use is higher, fertility is lower.

Notice that in this case the regression line slopes downward from left to right, rather than upward. That always indicates a negative correlation. And notice that a minus sign now precedes the correlation coefficient: −0.881**. This correlation is highly significant. And here we have data for 135 cases, with the data missing for 37.

The point of calculating correlation coefficients is not simply to say how alike or unalike two maps are. Indeed, the point of comparing two maps usually is not motivated by artistic concerns but, rather, in search of links, or connections, between variables. For only when such links exist can we propose that there is a causal relationship between them. No one would really think it is just an accident that there is an extremely high correlation between GDP per capita and automobile ownership. Rather, it seems likely that one is a cause of the other—that lack of income causes people not to own cars, while high incomes make it possible for them to do so. Nor would anyone suppose that fertility just happens to be low where contraceptive use is high; we assume that widespread use of contraceptives causes low fertility. In fact, whenever social scientists become interested in a variable, the first thing they usually ask is what causes it to vary. And the first test of any proposed answer to such a question is to demonstrate the existence of a correlation between the variable to be explained and its proposed cause. As will be discussed in detail in Exercise 15, by itself correlation does not establish that a causal relationship exists. But, *without a correlation there can be no causal relationship between two variables.*

Causation can be demonstrated by *either* a positive or a negative correlation. That is, an independent variable can cause a dependent variable to *increase*, resulting in a positive correlation as in the case of GDP per capita and cars per 1000. Or an independent variable can cause a dependent variable to *decrease*, as in the case of fertility and contraceptive use, hence a negative correlation.

Because you so often will be attempting to assess causal relations between variables, the scatterplot screen gives you the option to identify one variable as dependent and the other as independent. Of course, you can use the scatterplot feature to examine correlations even when you don't think two variables are causally related. In such cases, just ignore the designation of one as a dependent and the other as an independent variable.

Now let's try to test a cause-and-effect hypothesis. If one believes all of the concern expressed about trade imbalances, it would seem nations that import a lot will harm their economies—that imports cause slow growth:

Hypothesis: *Nations that import more will have a slower rate of economic growth.*

SCATTERPLOT:
    Dependent Variable: 39) GDP GROWTH
    Independent Variable: 40) IMPORTS

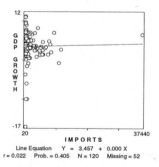

The hypothesis certainly sounded good, but it's not true. The relationship between these two variables is essentially random. The dots are scattered across the screen. The regression line has no slope and simply crosses the screen from left to right. The correlation coefficient is a minuscule −0.022, and there are no asterisks. Imports cannot cause slow economic growth, because the two variables are uncorrelated.

You will notice one case lying far to the right of the array. If you place the arrow on it and click you will discover that it is Singapore. The screen also will tell you what the correlation would be if Singapore were not included (0.062). But this is not significant either. The hypothesis must be rejected.

SCATTERPLOT:
   Dependent Variable: 15) FERTILITY
   Independent Variable: 11) TV SETS

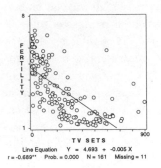

Line Equation   Y = 4.693 + -0.005 X
r = -0.689**   Prob. = 0.000   N = 161   Missing = 11

Here we see that there is a very strong and highly significant negative correlation between the fertility rate and the number of television sets per 1,000 population. A stand-up comic might want to suggest that this is a cause-and-effect relationship, but sociologists would not. Here we are reminded that correlation and causation are not the same thing. It is true that without correlation there can be no causation. But correlations often occur between two variables without one being a cause of the other. The correlation between contraceptive use and low fertility seems a legitimate example of a cause-and-effect relationship—use of contraception causes lower fertility. But the correlation shown just above is a clear example of a noncausal correlation. It is entirely implausible that television ownership, as such, would reduce fertility.

   OPEN FILE: STATES

   MAPPING: 43) PICKUPS

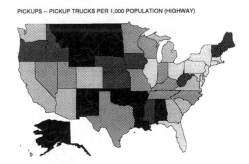

PICKUPS -- PICKUP TRUCKS PER 1,000 POPULATION (HIGHWAY)

This maps shows the number of pickup trucks per 1,000 population. Pickups are very regional, being most common in the western plains and the Rocky Mountain states.

Doing Sociology

RANK	CASE NAME	VALUE
1	Wyoming	231
2	Montana	208
3	Alabama	189
4	Arkansas	187
5	North Dakota	185
6	New Mexico	182
6	South Dakota	182
8	Oklahoma	178
9	Alaska	173
10	Louisiana	163

Wyoming is tops in terms of pickup trucks, having 231 per 1,000 population. Montana is second (208). Not surprisingly, New Jersey (48) and New York (43) have the lowest rates of pickup truck ownership.

COMPARING MAPS:
    Variable 1: 43) PICKUPS
    Variable 2: 28) FLD&STREAM

PICKUPS -- PICKUP TRUCKS PER 1,000 POPULATION (HIGHWAY)

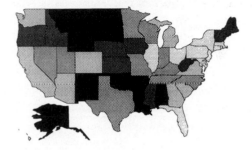

r = 0.808**

FLD&STREAM -- CIRCULATION OF FIELD & STREAM MAGAZINE PER 100,000 (ABC)

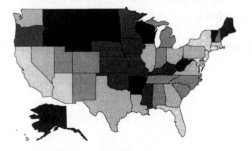

Now, rather than depend on visual comparisons to assess the similarity of these two maps, just look to the right of the screen: r = 0.808**. That's the correlation coefficient between the two maps. So, now you know. You always can discover the correlation between two maps either by doing a scatterplot or by comparing the maps. Both show precisely the same results, calculated in precisely the same way.

But simply to know there is a huge correlation between two variables does not tell us why. Clearly this is not an example of cause-and-effect. Pickup trucks neither subscribe to magazines nor do they cause their owners to subscribe.

What this correlation reflects is that lifestyles tend to be coherent—to fit together. Few people who drive pickup trucks also read *Gourmet* magazine or live in big cities. Instead, pickup truck owners read *Field & Stream* magazine and live in wide open spaces.

COMPARING MAPS:
      Variable 1: 43) PICKUPS
      Variable 2: 4) % METROPOL

PICKUPS -- PICKUP TRUCKS PER 1,000 POPULATION (HIGHWAY)

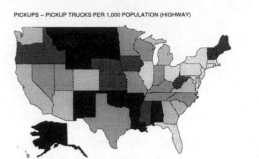

r = −0.811**

% METROPOL -- PERCENT OF POPULATION THAT RESIDES IN A METROPOLITAN STATISTICAL AREA (S.A.,1990)

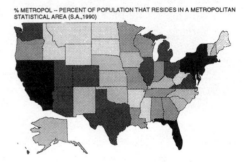

The lower map shows the percentage of the population in each state who live in metropolitan areas—big cities and their suburbs. The correlation is strong and negative (r = −0.811**). Pickups are not a big-city thing.

Your turn.

                                                          Doing Sociology

NAME: _____

COURSE: _____

DATE: _____

REVIEW QUESTIONS

Based on the first part of this exercise, answer True or False to the following items:

Nations that import more tend to have a slower rate of economic growth.   T   F

The regression line can show whether a correlation is positive or negative.   T   F

An independent variable is one we think is the cause of something.   T   F

A negative correlation proves there is no cause-and-effect relationship between
two variables.   T   F

Pearson used the letter n as the symbol for his correlation coefficient.   T   F

OPEN FILE: GLOBAL

1. **Hypothesis:** *Nations where cigarette consumption is higher will have a shorter average life expectancy.*

    SCATTERPLOT:
        DEPENDENT VARIABLE: 2) LIFE EXPEC
        INDEPENDENT VARIABLE: 10) CIGARETTES

    What is the value of r?   r = _____

    Is this a positive or negative correlation? (circle one)   Positive   Negative

    Is it statistically significant? (circle one)   Yes   No

    Is the hypothesis supported or rejected? (circle one)   Supported   Rejected

    Might this correlation reveal a cause-and-effect relationship?   Might be cause-and-effect
    Probably is not cause-and-effect
    No correlation

Briefly explain your answer about cause-and-effect.

_____

_____

_____

_____

_____

2. **Hypothesis:** *Nations where daily calorie consumption is higher will have a longer average life expectancy.*

   SCATTERPLOT:
   DEPENDENT VARIABLE: 2) LIFE EXPEC
   INDEPENDENT VARIABLE: 17) CALORIES

   What is the value of r?   r = _____

   Is this a positive or negative correlation? (circle one)   Positive   Negative

   Is it statistically significant? (circle one)   Yes   No

   Is the hypothesis supported or rejected? (circle one)   Supported   Rejected

   Might this correlation reveal a cause-and-effect relationship?   Might be cause-and-effect
                                                          Probably is not cause-and-effect
                                                                    No correlation

   Briefly explain your answer about cause-and-effect.

   _____

   _____

   _____

   _____

   _____

3. **Hypothesis:** *Nations where alcohol consumption is higher will have a longer average life expectancy.*

    SCATTERPLOT:
        DEPENDENT VARIABLE: 2) LIFE EXPEC
        INDEPENDENT VARIABLE: 28) ALCOHOL

    What is the value of r?   r = _____

    Is this a positive or negative correlation? (circle one)   Positive   Negative

    Is it statistically significant? (circle one)   Yes   No

    Is the hypothesis supported or rejected? (circle one)   Supported   Rejected

    Might this correlation reveal a cause-and-effect relationship?   **Might be cause-and-effect**
                                            Probably is not cause-and-effect
                                                  No correlation

   Briefly explain your answer about cause-and-effect.

   _____

   _____

   _____

   _____

   _____

4. **Hypothesis:** *Nations where drug use is higher will have a longer average life expectancy.*

    SCATTERPLOT:
        DEPENDENT VARIABLE: 2) LIFE EXPEC
        INDEPENDENT VARIABLE: 29) DRUG USE

    What is the value of r?   r = _____

    Is this a positive or negative correlation? (circle one)   Positive   Negative

    Is it statistically significant? (circle one)   Yes   No

    Is the hypothesis supported or rejected? (circle one)   Supported   Rejected

Might this correlation reveal a cause-and-effect relationship?

Might be cause-and-effect
Probably is not cause-and-effect
No correlation

Briefly explain your answer about cause-and-effect.

_____

_____

_____

_____

_____

5. **Hypothesis:** *Nations where more people believe in God will have lower suicide rates.*

    SCATTERPLOT:
       DEPENDENT VARIABLE: 51) SUICIDE
      INDEPENDENT VARIABLE: 36) GOD EXISTS

What is the value of r?   r = _____

Is this a positive or negative correlation? (circle one)   Positive   Negative

Is it statistically significant? (circle one)   Yes   No

Is the hypothesis supported or rejected? (circle one)   Supported   Rejected

Might this correlation reveal a cause-and-effect relationship?

Might be cause-and-effect
Probably is not cause-and-effect
No correlation

Briefly explain your answer about cause-and-effect.

_____

_____

_____

_____

_____

6. **Hypothesis:** *Nations that export more will have a higher economic growth rate.*

    SCATTERPLOT:
    DEPENDENT VARIABLE: 39) GDP GROWTH
    INDEPENDENT VARIABLE: 46) EXPORTS

    What is the value of r?   r = _____

    Is this a positive or negative correlation? (circle one)   Positive   Negative

    Is it statistically significant? (circle one)   Yes   No

    Is the hypothesis supported or rejected? (circle one)   Supported   Rejected

    Might this correlation reveal a cause-and-effect relationship?   Might be cause-and-effect
                                                                                          Probably is not cause-and-effect
                                                                                                          No correlation

    Briefly explain your answer about cause-and-effect.

    _____

    _____

    _____

    _____

    _____

    OPEN FILE: STATES

7. **Hypothesis:** *In states where more people own pickup trucks, alcohol consumption will be higher.*

    SCATTERPLOT:
    DEPENDENT VARIABLE: 19) ALCOHOL
    INDEPENDENT VARIABLE: 43) PICKUPS

    What is the value of r?   r = _____

    Is this a positive or negative correlation? (circle one)   Positive   Negative

    Is it statistically significant? (circle one)   Yes   No

Is the hypothesis supported or rejected? (circle one)   Supported   Rejected

Might this correlation reveal a cause-and-effect relationship?   Might be cause-and-effect
Probably is not cause-and-effect
No correlation

Briefly explain your answer about cause-and-effect.

_____

_____

_____

_____

_____

8.   **Hypothesis:** *In states where more people read* Playboy, *alcohol consumption will be higher.*

SCATTERPLOT:
   DEPENDENT VARIABLE: 19) ALCOHOL
   INDEPENDENT VARIABLE: 46) PLAYBOY

What is the value of r?   r = _____

Is this a positive or negative correlation? (circle one)   Positive   Negative

Is it statistically significant? (circle one)   Yes   No

Is the hypothesis supported or rejected? (circle one)   Supported   Rejected

Might this correlation reveal a cause-and-effect relationship?   Might be cause-and-effect
Probably is not cause-and-effect
No correlation

Briefly explain your answer about cause-and-effect.

_____

_____

_____

_____

_____

9. **Hypothesis:** *In states where more people read* Playboy, *there will be more divorces.*

    SCATTERPLOT:
        DEPENDENT VARIABLE: 20) %DIVORCED
        INDEPENDENT VARIABLE: 46) PLAYBOY

    What is the value of r?   r = _____

    Is this a positive or negative correlation? (circle one)   Positive   Negative

    Is it statistically significant? (circle one)   Yes   No

    Is the hypothesis supported or rejected? (circle one)   Supported   Rejected

    Might this correlation reveal a cause-and-effect relationship?   Might be cause-and-effect
                                      Probably is not cause-and-effect
                                          No correlation

Briefly explain your answer about cause-and-effect.

_____

_____

_____

_____

_____

10. **Hypothesis:** *In states where more people hunt, the circulation of* Field & Stream *magazine will be higher.*

    SCATTERPLOT:
        DEPENDENT VARIABLE: 28) FLD&STREAM
        INDEPENDENT VARIABLE: 27) HUNTERS

    What is the value of r?   r = _____

    Is this a positive or negative correlation? (circle one)   Positive   Negative

    Is it statistically significant? (circle one)   Yes   No

    Is the hypothesis supported or rejected? (circle one)   Supported   Rejected

Might this correlation reveal a cause-and-effect relationship?

Might be cause-and-effect
Probably is not cause-and-effect
No correlation

Briefly explain your answer about cause-and-effect.

_____

_____

_____

_____

_____

11. **Hypothesis:** *In states where the median family income is lower, the high school drop-out rate will be higher.*

    SCATTERPLOT:
        DEPENDENT VARIABLE: 33) DROP-OUTS
        INDEPENDENT VARIABLE: 7) MED.FAM$

What is the value of r?   r = _____

Is this a positive or negative correlation? (circle one)   Positive   Negative

Is it statistically significant? (circle one)   Yes   No

Is the hypothesis supported or rejected? (circle one)   Supported   Rejected

Might this correlation reveal a cause-and-effect relationship?

Might be cause-and-effect
Probably is not cause-and-effect
No correlation

Briefly explain your answer about cause-and-effect.

_____

_____

_____

_____

_____

12. **Hypothesis:** *In states where a higher percentage of people have college degrees, there will be more psychiatrists per 100,000 population.*

SCATTERPLOT:
     DEPENDENT VARIABLE: 25) SHRINKS
     INDEPENDENT VARIABLE: 35) COL.DEGREE

What is the value of r?   r = _____

Is this a positive or negative correlation? (circle one)   Positive   Negative

Is it statistically significant? (circle one)   Yes   No

Is the hypothesis supported or rejected? (circle one)   Supported   Rejected

Might this correlation reveal a cause-and-effect relationship?   Might be cause-and-effect
                                                Probably is not cause-and-effect
                                                       No correlation

Briefly explain your answer about cause-and-effect.

_____

_____

_____

_____

_____

EXERCISE 4:
SOCIALIZATION: GENDER ROLES

TASKS: Mapping, Univariate, Cross-tabulation
DATA FILES: GLOBAL, SURVEY

Anewborn infant understands very little of what is going on around it and, in that sense, is not yet a "person." It was only through a long period of interaction between us and other people that we became people too—a process called socialization. But socialization doesn't end in childhood. Instead, it is a lifelong process—as people shift from one major social role to another, they often undergo rather marked changes in outlook and behavior. In this exercise you will explore a major element in everyone's socialization: gender roles.

OPEN FILE: GLOBAL

Until very recently, the major aspects of male and female roles involved the primary responsibility for child care. Since only women can give birth or nurse an infant, it seemed obvious that they should stay home and take responsibility for raising the children. Even today, when the majority of mothers in the most economically developed nations hold full-time jobs outside the home, and mainly rely on day-care centers or other nonfamily persons for child care, there is considerable disagreement about whether that is an adequate substitute for the traditional stay-at-home mom.

MAPPING: 48) WORK WARM

WORK WARM -- PERCENT WHO AGREE THAT "A working mother can establish just as warm and secure a relationship with her children as a mother who does not

Here we see the percentage in each of the surveyed nations who agreed that "a working mother can establish just as warm and secure a relationship with her children as a mother who does not work."

LIST RANK

RANK	CASE NAME	VALUE
1	Finland	94
2	Taiwan	91
3	Japan	89
4	Romania	84
4	China	84
4	South Korea	84
7	Denmark	83
7	Estonia	83
9	Bosnia	82
9	Armenia	82

In Finland nearly everyone (94 percent) agreed. But agreement runs quite high nearly everywhere. In fact, only in three nations—Poland (49 percent), Turkey (49 percent), and Bangladesh (47 percent)—did fewer than half agree.

MAPPING: 47) SINGLE MOM

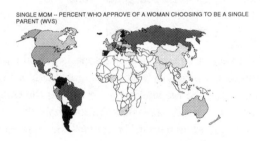

SINGLE MOM -- PERCENT WHO APPROVE OF A WOMAN CHOOSING TO BE A SINGLE PARENT (WVS)

This map shows the percentages who approve of a woman choosing to be a single parent.

LIST RANK

RANK	CASE NAME	VALUE
1	Iceland	84
2	Spain	75
3	Colombia	74
4	Lithuania	70
5	Slovenia	68
6	Denmark	67
7	Uruguay	66
7	Chile	66
9	Venezuela	64
10	Croatia	62

Although 84 percent agreed with this item in Iceland, in general approval runs lower—below 50 percent in more than half of the nations surveyed. In the United States only 40 percent approved, while in Nigeria, China, and India only 7 percent approved of single motherhood.

Of course, quite aside from attitudes concerning women and children is the simple issue of women's power. The social research staff of the United Nations has constructed an index of Gender

Empowerment based on the situation of women (compared with that of men) in the political and economic spheres of activity. The index is updated regularly to reflect changing circumstances.

MAPPING: 5) GENDER POW

GENDER POW -- INDEX OF EMPOWERMENT OF WOMEN (HDR)

Here is the map of the most recent Gender Empowerment index.

LIST RANK

RANK	CASE NAME	VALUE
1	Norway	0.825
2	Iceland	0.802
3	Sweden	0.794
4	Denmark	0.791
5	Finland	0.757
6	Germany	0.756
7	Netherlands	0.739
8	Canada	0.739
9	New Zealand	0.731
10	Belgium	0.725

The five nations with the highest scores are all in Scandinavia. The United States is thirteenth, just below Australia and Austria, and just ahead of Switzerland and the United Kingdom. Egypt, Jordan, and Niger have the lowest scores.

OPEN FILE: SURVEY

UNIVARIATE: 37) HOMEMAKER

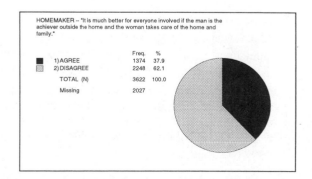

HOMEMAKER -- "It is much better for everyone involved if the man is the achiever outside the home and the woman takes care of the home and family."

	Freq.	%
1) AGREE	1374	37.9
2) DISAGREE	2248	62.1
TOTAL (N)	3622	100.0
Missing	2027	

This question measures traditional gender roles—the man as the breadwinner, the wife as the home-maker. Americans reject this outlook by a margin of nearly 2 to 1.

UNIVARIATE: 35) WORK WARM

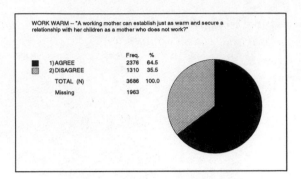

This item takes much the same point of view. Again, Americans believe that a working mother can be as close to her children as a nonworking mother by a margin of about 2 to 1.

Notice this is slightly less than than the 75 percent of Americans who agreed in the World Values Surveys as reported in the GLOBAL data file above. There are several probable reasons for this difference. First, these GSS surveys were conducted several years later than the one for the WVS and opinions may have shifted some. Second, the WVS survey was by a different organization with different sampling points. And of course, there will be differences between surveys on the basis of random fluctuations.

CROSS-TABULATION:
Row Variable: 35) WORK WARM
Column Variable: 1) YEAR
Column %

WORK WARM by YEAR
Cramer's V: 0.070 **

		YEAR		TOTAL
		2000	1998	TOTAL
WORK WARM	AGREE	1128	1248	2376
		61.1%	67.8%	64.5%
	DISAGREE	718	592	1310
		38.9%	32.2%	35.5%
	Missing	971	992	1963
	TOTAL	1846	1840	3686
		100.0%	100.0%	

Here we see a substantial fluctuation in the proportion who agreed between those interviewed in 2000 (61.1 percent) and in 1998 (67.8 percent). The difference is significant. It still could be due entirely to random fluctuation since significance tells us only the *odds* that a difference is not purely random. Thus, if the odds are 100 to 1, that means on average there will be a difference this large purely by chance once in every 100 instances. This could have been the one. But it also could be that public attitudes shifted slightly on this issue during the two years between samples.

Thus far we have been examining sex role attitudes. But of even greater importance are sex roles themselves.

Three very primary sex roles are: (1) men employed full time; (2) women employed full time; and (3) women who are full-time housewives. To make the three groups comparable, everyone age 65 and over has been omitted. This results in 1,603 working men, 1,437 working women, and 461 housewives (excluded are those working only part time, students, the unemployed, the retired, and everyone over 64).

Hypothesis: *Housewives will differ greatly from working women in terms of their acceptance of traditional beliefs about gender roles.*

CROSS-TABULATION:
   Row Variable: 37) HOMEMAKER
  Column Variable: 16) SEX ROLES
     Column %

HOMEMAKER by SEX ROLES
Cramer's V: 0.171 **

		SEX ROLES				
		WORK MEN	WORK WOMEN	HOUSEWIVES	Missing	TOTAL
HOMEMAKER	AGREE	354	226	149	645	729
		34.5%	24.2%	48.2%		32.1%
	DISAGREE	673	707	160	708	1540
		65.5%	75.8%	51.8%		67.9%
	Missing	576	504	152	795	2027
	TOTAL	1027	933	309	2148	2269
		100.0%	100.0%	100.0%		

Working women overwhelmingly disagreed (75.8 percent) with this question. But so did the majority of housewives (51.8 percent). While the difference is significant and supports the hypothesis, the fact that most housewives did disagree should make us cautious about assuming that housewives "differ greatly" from working women in terms of their commitment to very traditional sex role views.

CROSS-TABULATION:
   Row Variable: 35) WORK WARM
  Column Variable: 16) SEX ROLES
     Column %

WORK WARM by SEX ROLES
Cramer's V: 0.206 **

		SEX ROLES				
		WORK MEN	WORK WOMEN	HOUSEWIVES	Missing	TOTAL
WORK WARM	AGREE	605	732	194	845	1531
		57.4%	78.0%	61.4%		66.3%
	DISAGREE	449	207	122	532	778
		42.6%	22.0%	38.6%		33.7%
	Missing	549	498	145	771	1963
	TOTAL	1054	939	316	2148	2309
		100.0%	100.0%	100.0%		

Here too housewives are a bit less likely than working women to agree that a working mother can establish as warm a relationship with her children as can a housewife. But of perhaps more importance is that the difference is that the overwhelming majority of housewives did agree. This serves to remind us that sociological research isn't just a matter of confirming the obvious. Most hypotheses turn out to be wrong or to be true only to a very modest degree! And that's what makes the search for important factors so much fun.

Now let's shift from attitudes to activities.

Hypothesis: *Because they have more leisure time, housewives are more apt to read fiction than are working men and women.*

CROSS-TABULATION:
Row Variable: 44) READER?
Column Variable: 16) SEX ROLES
Column %

READER? by SEX ROLES
Cramer's V: 0.167 **

		SEX ROLES				
		WORK MEN	WORK WOMEN	HOUSEWIVES	Missing	TOTAL
READER?	YES	275	278	85	330	638
		62.5%	79.0%	70.8%		70.0%
	NO	165	74	35	192	274
		37.5%	21.0%	29.2%		30.0%
	Missing	1163	1085	341	1626	4215
	TOTAL	440	352	120	2148	912
		100.0%	100.0%	100.0%		

Housewives are more likely to read fiction than are working men, but they are less likely to do so than are working women. Because not everyone was asked about reading, the difference between working women and housewives is based on a small number of cases and might not be significant—the significant difference reflected by the asterisks might be only the one between men and women. To find out, let's limit the table to women.

CROSS-TABULATION:
Row Variable: 44) READER?
Column Variable: 39) WORK/HOUSE
Column %

READER? by WORK/HOUSE
Cramer's V: 0.084

		WORK/HOUSE			
		WORK WOMEN	HOUSEWIVES	Missing	TOTAL
READER?	YES	278	85	605	363
		79.0%	70.8%		76.9%
	NO	74	35	357	109
		21.0%	29.2%		23.1%
	Missing	1085	341	2789	4215
	TOTAL	352	120	3751	472
		100.0%	100.0%		

Here we see that the difference between working women and housewives is not significant. The proper interpretation is simply that men are less apt than women to read fiction.

Your turn.

Doing Sociology

WORKSHEET

NAME: _Bill Sanda_

COURSE: _____

DATE: _____

EXERCISE
4

REVIEW QUESTIONS

Based on the first part of this exercise, answer True or False to the following items:

The socialization process lasts until about the age of 10.	T	F
Significance tests rule out any possibility that a difference occurred by random fluctuation.	T	F
American housewives overwhelmingly hold traditional notions about sex roles.	T	F
There are far more women who work full-time than there are full-time housewives.	T	F
Working women are significantly less likely than housewives to read fiction.	T	F

OPEN FILE: SURVEY

1. **Hypothesis:** *Men would be less willing than women to vote for a woman running for President of the United States.*

CROSS-TABULATION:
    ROW VARIABLE: 38) FEM.PREZ
  COLUMN VARIABLE: 3) SEX
         Column %

Copy the first row of the percentaged table:

SEX

	MALE	FEMALE
YES	_____%	_____%

What is the value of V for this table?   V = _____

Is V statistically significant?   Yes   No

Is the hypothesis supported or rejected?   Supported   Rejected

Exercise 4: Socialization: Gender Roles   63

How would you explain this finding? Express yourself without worrying about giving a "wrong" answer.

_____

_____

_____

_____

_____

2.   **Hypothesis:** *Men are more likely than women to think that men should be the achievers outside the home.*

CROSS-TABULATION:
   ROW VARIABLE: 37) HOMEMAKER
   COLUMN VARIABLE: 3) SEX
          Column %

Copy the first row of the percentaged table:

SEX
                          MALE   **FEMALE**

     YES   _____%   _____%

What is the value of V for this table?   V = _____

Is V statistically significant?   Yes   No

Is the hypothesis supported or rejected?   Supported   Rejected

How would you explain this finding? Express yourself without worrying about giving a "wrong" answer.

_____

_____

_____

_____

_____

3. **Hypothesis:** *Working men and women are more likely to have extramarital sex than are housewives.*

CROSS-TABULATION:
> **ROW VARIABLE:** 21) UNFAITHFUL
> **COLUMN VARIABLE:** 16) SEX ROLES
> **Column %**

Copy the first row of the percentaged table:

ROLES	**WORKING MEN**	**WORKING WOMEN**	**HOUSEWIVES**
CHEATED	_____%	_____%	_____%

Which group is most apt to have been unfaithful?   _____

Which group is least apt to have been unfaithful?   _____

What is the value of V for this table?   V = _____

Is V statistically significant?   Yes   No

Is the hypothesis supported or rejected?   Supported   Rejected

How would you explain this finding? Express yourself without worrying about giving a "wrong" answer.

_____

_____

_____

_____

_____

4. **Hypothesis:** *Working women will have had more sex partners recently than will housewives.*

CROSS-TABULATION:
> **ROW VARIABLE:** 24) #SEX PARTN
> **COLUMN VARIABLE:** 39) WORK/HOUSE
> **Column %**

Copy the first row of the percentaged table:

WORK/HOUSE

	WORKING WOMEN	HOUSEWIVES
3 OR MORE	_____%	_____%

What is the value of V for this table?   V = _____

Is V statistically significant?   Yes   No

Is the hypothesis supported or rejected?   Supported   Rejected

How would you explain this finding? Express yourself without worrying about giving a "wrong" answer.

_____

_____

_____

_____

_____

5. **Hypothesis:** *Working women will have sex more often than will housewives.*

CROSS-TABULATION:
    ROW VARIABLE: 23) SEX OFTEN?
COLUMN VARIABLE: 39) WORK/HOUSE
       Column %

Copy the first row of the percentaged table:

WORK/HOUSE

	WORKING WOMEN	HOUSEWIVES
WEEKLY	_____%	_____%

What is the value of V for this table?   V = _____

Is V statistically significant?   Yes   No

Is the hypothesis supported or rejected?   Supported   Rejected

How would you explain this finding? Express yourself without worrying about giving a "wrong" answer.

_____

_____

_____

_____

_____

6. **Hypothesis:** *Housewives will have more children than will women with full-time jobs.*

CROSS-TABULATION:
ROW VARIABLE: 32) # KIDS
COLUMN VARIABLE: 39) WORK/HOUSE
Column %

Copy the first and fourth rows of the percentaged table:

WORK/HOUSE

	WORKING WOMEN	HOUSEWIVES
NONE	_____%	_____%
4 OR MORE	_____%	_____%

What is the value of V for this table?   V = _____

Is V statistically significant?   Yes   No

Is the hypothesis supported or rejected?   Supported   Rejected

How would you explain this finding? Express yourself without worrying about giving a "wrong" answer.

_____

_____

_____

_____

_____

7. **Hypothesis:** *Working men and women are less likely to have happy marriages than are housewives.*

CROSS-TABULATION:
    ROW VARIABLE: 22) HAPPY MAR?
   COLUMN VARIABLE: 16) SEX ROLES
       Column %

Copy the first row of the percentaged table:

ROLES

	WORKING MEN	WORKING WOMEN	HOUSEWIVES
VERY HAPPY	_____%	_____%	_____%

Which group is most apt to have a happy marriage?   _____

Which group is least apt to have a happy marriage?   _____

What is the value of V for this table?   V = _____

Is V statistically significant?   Yes   No

Is the hypothesis supported or rejected?   Supported   Rejected

How would you explain this finding? Express yourself without worrying about giving a "wrong" answer.

_____

_____

_____

_____

_____

8. **Hypothesis:** *Working men and women watch less television than do housewives.*

CROSS-TABULATION:
    ROW VARIABLE: 41) TV TIME
   COLUMN VARIABLE: 16) SEX ROLES
       Column %

Copy the first row of the percentaged table:

ROLES			
	WORKING MEN	WORKING WOMEN	HOUSEWIVES
3 OR MORE	_____%	_____%	_____%

Which group watches the most TV?   _____

Which group watches the least TV?   _____

What is the value of V for this table?   V = _____

Is V statistically significant?   Yes   No

Is the hypothesis supported or rejected?   Supported   Rejected

9. **Hypothesis:** *Working men and women go to movies less often than do housewives.*

CROSS-TABULATION:
    ROW VARIABLE: 43) GO 2 MOVIE
COLUMN VARIABLE: 16) SEX ROLES
        Column %

Copy the first row of the percentaged table:

ROLES			
	WORKING MEN	WORKING WOMEN	HOUSEWIVES
YES	_____%	_____%	_____%

Which group is most apt to have been to a movie?   _____

Which group is least apt to have been to a movie?   _____

What is the value of V for this table?   V = _____

Is V statistically significant?   Yes   No

Is the hypothesis supported or rejected?   Supported   Rejected

How would you explain this finding? Express yourself without worrying about giving a "wrong" answer.

_____

_____

_____

_____

_____

10. **Hypothesis:** *Working men and women go to bars and taverns more often than do housewives.*

CROSS-TABULATION:
    ROW VARIABLE: 46) GO 2 BARS
  COLUMN VARIABLE: 16) SEX ROLES
      Column %

Copy the first and fourth rows of the percentaged table:

ROLES	WORKING MEN	WORKING WOMEN	HOUSEWIVES
WEEKLY +	_____%	_____%	_____%
NEVER	_____%	_____%	_____%

Which group is most apt to go to a bar weekly or more often? _____

Which group is most apt to never go to a bar? _____

What is the value of V for this table?   V = _____

Is V statistically significant?   Yes   No

Is the hypothesis supported or rejected?   Supported   Rejected

How would you explain this finding? Express yourself without worrying about giving a "wrong"" answer.

_____

_____

_____

_____

_____

11. **Hypothesis:** *Working men and women are less likely to have seen a doctor in the past week than are housewives.*

CROSS-TABULATION:
    ROW VARIABLE: 45) GO 2 DOC?
  COLUMN VARIABLE: 16) SEX ROLES
      Column %

Copy the first row of the percentaged table:

ROLES	**WORKING MEN**	**WORKING WOMEN**	**HOUSEWIVES**
YES	_____%	_____%	_____%

Which group is most apt to have been to a doctor?   _____

Which group is least apt to have been to a doctor?   _____

What is the value of V for this table?   V = _____

Is V statistically significant?   Yes   No

Is the hypothesis supported or rejected?   Supported   Rejected

CROSS-TABULATION:
    ROW VARIABLE: 45) GO 2 DOC?
  COLUMN VARIABLE: 39) WORK/HOUSE
      Column %

Is the difference between working women and housewives significant?   Yes   No

How would you explain this finding? Express yourself without worrying about giving a "wrong" answer.

_____

_____

_____
_____
_____

12. On the basis of what you have found out in this exercise, compare the lives of housewives and working women.

_____
_____
_____
_____
_____
_____
_____
_____
_____
_____
_____
_____
_____
_____
_____
_____
_____
_____
_____

EXERCISE 5:
DEVIANCE

> **TASKS:** Mapping, Correlation, Univariate, Cross-Tabulation
> **DATA FILES:** GLOBAL, STATES, SURVEY, COUNTIES

The nineteenth-century founders of sociology agreed that modernization was at best a very mixed blessing—that the new conditions of life would be corrosive of social solidarity, the strong interpersonal bonds uniting members of a community. As solidarity weakened, the result would be a world of unattached strangers, many of whom would engage in antisocial behavior. In contrast with life in small villages, where everyone was known to everyone else and thus constrained by emotional bonds and by close surveillance to obey the norms, in the rapidly growing industrial cities people would be free to break the norms.

At the start of the twentieth century, the French sociologist Emile Durkheim formulated a theory linking social disorganization and social pathology, thus encompassing these fears about the negative effects of modernization. **Social disorganization** is defined as all of those factors that produce weaknesses in social solidarity, the network of social relations linking individuals to one another. Examples include high rates of migration and geographic mobility, which result in "communities" of strangers. **Social pathology** is defined as deviant behavior, including suicide, crime, and substance abuse. Durkheim's theory that social disorganization causes social pathology is a form of control theory—the approach to deviance that asks not why some people deviate but, rather, why everyone doesn't break the norms. That is, Durkheim and other control theorists assume that everyone has sufficient motives to violate the norms (to, for example, steal things they want), so control theorists focus on what prevents (or controls) most of us from doing so, at least most of the time. And they reason that one thing that prevents most of us from committing deviant acts is our concern to retain the respect of our family and friends. People lacking such attachments will not have such concerns and therefore will have less to lose by being detected in deviant behavior. In this sense, deviance is the expected behavior when social controls are weak.

> **OPEN FILE:** GLOBAL

In order to test Durkheim's theory, we first need to select appropriate measures of social pathology.

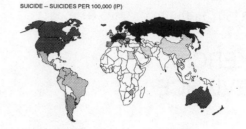

SUICIDE -- SUICIDES PER 100,000 (IP)

Here we see the world map of suicide rates.

LIST RANK

RANK	CASE NAME	VALUE
1	Hungary	42.6
2	Sri Lanka	30.0
3	Finland	29.9
4	Denmark	26.6
5	Austria	23.1
6	Belgium	22.3
7	Switzerland	21.0
8	Russia	20.8
9	France	19.8
10	Luxembourg	18.6

Hungary (42.6) has the highest rate. Of the highest 15, all but Sri Lanka are European nations. Of the 10 nations with the lowest rates, 6 are Islamic societies.

Suicide is, of course, a classic instance of social pathology—Durkheim devoted an entire book to suicide. But there are several other possible measures of social pathology in the GLOBAL data file.

CORRELATION:
Select Variables: 51) SUICIDE
28) ALCOHOL
29) DRUG USE
22) ABORTION
9) %WITH AIDS

Correlation Coefficients
PAIRWISE deletion (1-tailed test)   Significance Levels: ** =.01, * =.05

	SUICIDE	ALCOHOL	DRUG USE	ABORTION	%WITH AIDS
SUICIDE	1.000 (69)	0.526 ** (40)	0.409 ** (58)	0.268 (25)	-0.125 (67)
ALCOHOL	0.526 ** (40)	1.000 (48)	0.327 * (44)	-0.125 (26)	-0.061 (47)
DRUG USE	0.409 ** (58)	0.327 * (44)	1.000 (80)	-0.141 (28)	-0.074 (74)
ABORTION	0.268 (25)	-0.125 (26)	-0.141 (28)	1.000 (28)	-0.251 (27)
%WITH AIDS	-0.125 (67)	-0.061 (47)	-0.074 (74)	-0.251 (27)	1.000 (152)

This display is called a *correlation matrix*. It shows the correlation between each of these four variables. It can be read either by finding a variable up the left side and reading across, or by finding it across the top and reading down. Here the correlation between suicide and alcohol consumption is 0.526**, and highly significant (see the two asterisks). The correlation between suicide and drug use is 0.409**, and between alcohol and drugs, 0.327*. However, there are no significant correlations between the percent with AIDS and any of the other variables. Nor is the abortion rate correlated significantly with suicide, alcohol, or drug use.

If variables are measures of the same thing, they will be correlated. That standard is met by suicide, drug use, and alcohol consumption. Each correlation strengthens the assumption that all three measure social pathology. But it is equally clear that neither AIDS nor abortion should be used as a measure of social pathology. However, although things that measure the same thing must be correlated, that does not mean that just because two variables are correlated they do measure the same thing. Life expectancy and TV sets are correlated, but they surely are not the same thing. In fact, of course, causes must be correlated with their effects, but causes and effects are not the same thing either. So, in addition to checking to see if two things are correlated, in order to claim they are measures of the same thing requires reason and logic: arguments about why they are similar. On those grounds, too, one might well conclude that abortion and AIDS rates differ substantially from suicide, alcohol, and drug abuse rates.

Durkheim developed his theory late in the nineteenth century, during a time of rapid modernization and economic development. As noted, at that time all sociologists were very worried that these changes were tearing down the fabric of social relationships that had bound people in villages and rural areas to the moral order. Therefore, Durkheim would have agreed with this hypothesis: *Suicide, alcohol, and drug use will be positively correlated with GDP per capita.*

CORRELATION:
Select Variables: 3) $ GDP/CAP
51) SUICIDE
28) ALCOHOL
29) DRUG USE

Correlation Coefficients
PAIRWISE deletion (1-tailed test)   Significance Levels: ** =.01, * =.05

	$ GDP/CAP	SUICIDE	ALCOHOL	DRUG USE
$ GDP/CAP	1.000 (171)	0.405 ** (69)	0.606 ** (48)	0.623 ** (80)
SUICIDE	0.405 ** (69)	1.000 (69)	0.526 ** (40)	0.409 ** (58)
ALCOHOL	0.606 ** (48)	0.526 ** (40)	1.000 (48)	0.327 * (44)
DRUG USE	0.623 ** (80)	0.409 ** (58)	0.327 * (44)	1.000 (80)

As predicted, all of the correlations are strong, highly significant, and positive. These forms of social pathology do tend to afflict the wealthier, more developed nations.

Durkheim also regarded crime as a major kind of social pathology. The most common crime rates are based on official statistics provided by the police. Thus these rates consist only of those crimes known to the police—many crimes go unreported and do not show up in these statistics. In the past few years, official crime statistics have been reported for a number of nations. A second source of crime statistics is large surveys asking people about crimes committed against them during a specific period, usually the past year. These are known as victimization surveys. These studies were pioneered in the United States and now are available for several other nations.

However, no crime statistics have been included in the GLOBAL data file. The reason is that international crime statistics are suspect and often incomparable because of variations in the willingness of people to report crimes to the police and in how particular crime categories are defined. For example, some nations include attempted murders in their homicide rates, others do not. Some classify traffic deaths caused by drunk drivers as homicide, others do not. In the past decade a great deal of effort has been devoted to establishing common definitions for various crimes. But even common definitions do not overcome the major international variations created by differences in reporting. For example, in the most recent international statistics (*U.N. Human Development Report, 2000*), there were 463.6 rapes reported per 100,000 women aged 15 and over in Estonia, 267.3 in Canada, and 199.1 in Iceland. In contrast, the reported rate for Great Britain was 3.0, New Zealand's rate was 3.4 and Spain's was 7.2. Differences of such magnitude are obviously nonsense. Whether the differences stem from different definitions or differences in the willingness of victims to call the police, hardly matters. What matters is that rates so obviously flawed are unusable for research.

In contrast, data on suicide and drug use do not depend on notification of the police, but originate with public health departments and seem quite reliable. Alcohol consumption is very accurate since all nations tax alcohol and thus know precisely how much is sold each year.

In any event, to test Durkheim's theory using crime statistics, we will need to use data based on the United States.

OPEN FILE: STATES

Durkheim's theory is not specific to nations. Even within nations, social pathology should vary in response to variations in social disorganization. We can use the suicide rate to measure social pathology, and for states we have far more direct measures of social disorganization than are available for nations. Population instability is one such measure. The more often that people move, the higher the percentage of a population that consists of newcomers and strangers.

CORRELATION:

Select Variables: 11) % MOVERS
23) CRIME INDEX

Correlation Coefficients
PAIRWISE deletion (1-tailed test)   Significance Levels: ** = .01, * = .05

	% MOVERS	CRIME INDX
% MOVERS	1.000 (50)	0.415 ** (50)
CRIME INDX	0.415 ** (50)	1.000 (50)

The crime index is the total number of crimes of all major types per 100,000 population. It is highly correlated with the percentage in each state who have moved during the past five years. This supports Durkheim. What about suicide?

CORRELATION:

Select Variables: 11) % MOVERS
22) SUICIDE

Correlation Coefficients
PAIRWISE deletion (1-tailed test)   Significance Levels: ** = .01, * = .05

	% MOVERS	SUICIDE
% MOVERS	1.000 (50)	0.609 ** (50)
SUICIDE	0.609 ** (50)	1.000 (50)

Again, Durkheim is supported by a high correlation.

OPEN FILE: SURVEY

Now, let's try something different.

UNIVARIATE: 47) MOVERS

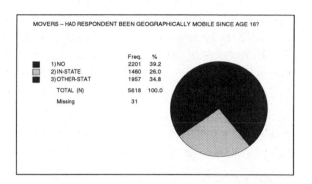

MOVERS -- HAD RESPONDENT BEEN GEOGRAPHICALLY MOBILE SINCE AGE 16?

	Freq.	%
1) NO	2201	39.2
2) IN-STATE	1460	26.0
3) OTHER-STAT	1957	34.8
TOTAL (N)	5618	100.0
Missing	31	

Here we see that many Americans are geographically mobile. While 39.2 percent have not left the town in which they lived when they were 16, about one-fourth (26.0 percent) have moved to a different place within the same state in which they grew up, and about a third (34.8 percent) now live in a different state. Can we interpret Durkheim as assuming that people who move are more apt to be victims of social disorganization? If so, then we would hypothesize that they would be more apt to commit acts of deviance. The only possible measure of deviance available in the SURVEY data file is being unfaithful to one's spouse. Let's see if they are related.

CROSS-TABULATION:
 Row Variable: 21) UNFAITHFUL
 Column Variable: 47) MOVERS
 Column %

UNFAITHFUL by MOVERS
Cramer's V: 0.016

		MOVERS				
		NO	IN-STATE	OTHER-STAT	Missing	TOTAL
UNFAITHFUL	CHEATED	226	164	241	1	631
		18.0%	17.1%	18.6%		18.0%
	NOT	1033	796	1055	15	2884
		82.0%	82.9%	81.4%		82.0%
	Missing	942	500	661	15	2118
	TOTAL	1259	960	1296	31	3515
		100.0%	100.0%	100.0%		

There is no correlation at all! This helps remind us that Durkheim was theorizing about "social facts." Recall from Exercise 1 that social facts are *properties of groups*, not individuals. There is no way to know whether people who move are thereby subjected to the strains of social disorganization. Many of them may become firmly attached to many other people in their new location. What Durkheim was concerned about was that in *places* where there is a lot of coming and going, a higher proportion of people will be unattached than in places where everyone stays put. That is a social fact. Put another way, individuals do not have social facts, only groups do.

Your turn.

WORKSHEET

NAME:

COURSE:

DATE:

EXERCISE
5

REVIEW QUESTIONS

Based on the first part of this exercise, answer True or False to the following items:

Social disorganization refers to various forms of deviant behavior.	T	F
Suicide is higher in Islamic nations than in Europe.	T	F
If variables measure the same thing, then they will be correlated.	T	F
International crime statistics are not reliable.	T	F
Suicide rates are not correlated with the percentage of people who have moved.	T	F

OPEN FILE: GLOBAL

1. **Hypothesis:** *All valid measures of modernization (hence, of social disorganization) will be correlated.*

   CORRELATION:
   SELECT VARIABLE: 3) $ GDP/CAP
   53) ELECTRIC
   26) CARS/1000
   11) TV SETS
   39) GDP GROWTH

   Circle any variable(s) which should not be used as a measure of modernization and therefore of social disorganization.

2. **Hypothesis:** *Any valid measure of social disorganization will be correlated with any valid measure of social pathology.*

   From what you have learned so far, select two measures of modernization (*other than* $ GDP/CAP) and two measures of social pathology (*other than* SUICIDE), and create the appropriate correlation matrix.

   CORRELATION:
   SELECT VARIABLE: Your choice of two modernization measures
   Your choice of two social pathology measures

Fill in the correlation matrix:

	1.	2.	3.	4.
1.				
2.				
3.				
4.				

Is the hypothesis supported?   Yes   No

Explain your selections:

_____

_____

_____

_____

     OPEN FILE: STATES

3.   **Hypothesis:** *All valid measures of social disorganization will be correlated.*

     CORRELATION:
SELECT VARIABLE: 9) % STAYERS
             10) POP GROW
             4) % METROPOL
             11) % MOVERS
             17) BEER
             12) %NEWCOMERS
             26) ASTROLOGER

On the basis of correlations alone, which variable(s) should not be considered a measure of social disorganization?

LIST: _____

On the basis of reason and logic, are there any variables that should not be considered a measure of social disorganization?

LIST: _____

Explain your selections.

_____

_____

_____

_____

_____

4. **Hypothesis:** *The higher a state's rate of population growth, the higher its crime rate.*

    CORRELATION:
    SELECT VARIABLE: 10) POP GROW
                                    23) CRIME INDX

    What is the value of the correlation coefficient?   _____

    Is this a positive or a negative correlation?   Positive   Negative

    Is it statistically significant?   Yes   No

    Is the hypothesis supported or rejected?   Supported   Rejected

    Would you say this was a valid test of Durkheim's theory? Explain.

    _____

    _____

    _____

    _____

    _____

5. **Hypothesis:** *The higher a state's astrologer rate, the higher its suicide rate.*

    CORRELATION:
    SELECT VARIABLE: 26) ASTROLOGER
                                    22) SUICIDE

    What is the value of the correlation coefficient?   _____

Exercise 5: Deviance

Is this a positive or a negative correlation?   Positive   Negative

Is it statistically significant?   Yes   No

Is the hypothesis supported or rejected?   Supported   Rejected

Would you say this was a valid test of Durkheim's theory? Explain.

_____

_____

_____

_____

_____

6.   **Hypothesis:** *The higher the percentage of a state's population that lives in metropolitan areas, the higher its suicide rate.*

   CORRELATION:
   SELECT VARIABLE: 4) % METROPOL
                         22) SUICIDE

   What is the value of the correlation coefficient?   _____

   Is this a positive or a negative correlation?   Positive   Negative

   Is it statistically significant?   Yes   No

   Is the hypothesis supported or rejected?   Supported   Rejected

   Would you say this was a valid test of Durkheim's theory? Explain.

   _____

   _____

   _____

   _____

   _____

   OPEN FILE: COUNTIES

7. **Hypothesis:** *There will be a negative correlation between the percentage who have not moved and the crime rate.*

> **CORRELATION:**
> **SELECT VARIABLE:** 13) CRIME RATE
>   14) NOT MOVED

What is the value of the correlation coefficient?   _____

Is this a positive or a negative correlation?   Positive   Negative

Is it statistically significant?   Yes   No

Is the hypothesis supported or rejected?   Supported   Rejected

Would you say this was a valid test of Durkheim's theory? Explain.

_____

_____

_____

_____

_____

EXERCISE 6:
STRATIFICATION

TASKS: Mapping, Univariate
DATA FILES: XCULT, GLOBAL

Ⓐll known human societies have been **stratified**: some people have enjoyed greater material and social benefits than others. What has varied over the millennia is the degree of stratification. In some societies the gap between the top and bottom is quite small; in others it is immense—as between slaves laboring under the overseer's whip and aristocrats living lives of incredible privilege and luxury.

OPEN FILE: XCULT

For several centuries, travelers, missionaries, diplomats, anthropologists, and other social scientists have been writing reports about human cultures. Much of the emphasis has been on recording detailed accounts of the culture of preliterate societies in an effort to preserve this information before the group was destroyed or its original culture changed beyond recognition through contacts with more developed societies.

Early anthropologists and sociologists often used some of these materials to compare several societies. However, as a large number of studies of different cultures began to accumulate, some social scientists recognized that comparative studies would be far more conclusive if they could be based on many cases and subjected to statistical methods of analysis. To do this, however, required that the many written reports be transformed into sets of numerical values. For example, each of the reports acknowledged that the culture in question was stratified. But *how* stratified? Or how *much more* stratified, if at all, were the Aztecs than the Incas, or the Pawnees than the Comanches? In the case of modern societies we can measure stratification with a fair degree of numerical precision—for example, how much more income goes to the richest people than to the poorest? But when groups do not have a money economy, stratification is much harder to measure. So, as they coded data on these 186 societies making up the Standard Cross-Cultural Sample, a group of scholars at Yale University, working under the direction of George Peter Murdock, adopted a simple set of rules to classify each society into one of three levels of stratification: low, medium, and high.

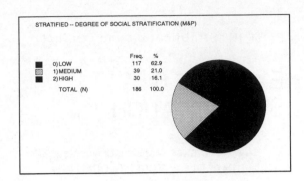

STRATIFIED -- DEGREE OF SOCIAL STRATIFICATION (M&P)

	Freq.	%
0)LOW	117	62.9
1)MEDIUM	39	21.0
2)HIGH	30	16.1
TOTAL (N)	186	100.0

Here we see the results. Most societies (62.9 percent) were coded as low in terms of their degree of stratification, 21.0 percent were coded as medium, and 16.1 percent were coded as high (including both the Aztecs and the Incas). Clearly, this coding is somewhat inexact in that there probably are differences in the actual degree of stratification of societies within the same group. But it is doubtful that any society is in the wrong category—that a society coded low, for example, is as stratified as the least stratified group placed in the medium category.

As feared, very few of these societies still exist and some have not existed for centuries. Thus, for example, when you map a variable in this data set, you will see that there are many of them scattered across North America. These are native American societies, and the information on their cultures was gathered a century or two ago. For that reason, in discussing these data, we will use the past tense—even though some of these societies do still exist.

MAPPING: 4) STRATIFIED

STRATIFIED -- DEGREE OF SOCIAL STRATIFICATION (M&P)

Remember that on this map each society is a dot. Looking at the dots, we easily can see that the dark dots tend to be clustered around the Mediterranean Sea. These dark dots represent the classic agrarian empires such as Egypt and Rome, which were among the most stratified societies in history.

Now let's examine factors that may affect stratification.

COMPARING MAPS:
  Variable 1: 4) STRATIFIED
  Variable 2: 11) GATHER

STRATIFIED -- DEGREE OF SOCIAL STRATIFICATION (M&P)

r = −0.365**

GATHER -- DEPENDENCE ON GATHERING FOR SUBSISTENCE (M&M)

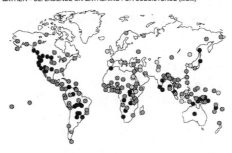

The significant, *negative* correlation between these two maps reveals that the degree of stratification tends to be shaped by how much wealth *anyone* can acquire. To the extent that a society depends on gathering for its subsistence, no one will be able to have much of anything and stratification will tend to be limited to modest differences in power and prestige based on age and gender.

COMPARING MAPS:
  Variable 1: 4) STRATIFIED
  Variable 2: 8) FIXITY

STRATIFIED -- DEGREE OF SOCIAL STRATIFICATION (M&P)

r = 0.431**

Exercise 6: Stratification

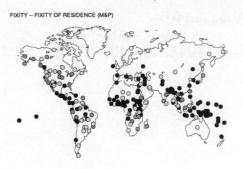

Fixity refers to the extent to which a society stays put. Many of these societies were quite nomadic, moving frequently, often in pursuit of game. The positive correlation reflects that if people cannot possess more than they can take with them on their backs or on pack animals (few of these societies possessed the wheel and none of the nomadic ones did), no one will have a lot of stuff.

COMPARING MAPS:
      Variable 1: 4) STRATIFIED
      Variable 2: 2) WRITING

STRATIFIED -- DEGREE OF SOCIAL STRATIFICATION (M&P)

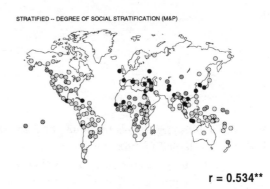

r = 0.534**

WRITING -- DO THEY HAVE A WRITTEN LANGUAGE? (M&P)

Societies that have a written language tend to be more stratified than societies without writing.

COMPARING MAPS:
       Variable 1: 4) STRATIFIED
       Variable 2: 14) C.COMPLEX

STRATIFIED -- DEGREE OF SOCIAL STRATIFICATION (M&P)

r = 0.624**

C.COMPLEX. -- LEVEL OF CULTURAL COMPLEXITY: METAL, DAIRY, STATE, DON'T HUNT

Cultural complexity sums up many aspects of a culture to identify societies as having more or less complex (advanced) cultures.

These results support the conclusion that *there is a tendency for societies to be more stratified, the wealthier they are.* In a sense, the relative equality of the societies with the least complex cultures is the equality of poverty—no one has much. But, as these societies become more productive, some people end up with a lot and others with very little.

COMPARING MAPS:
       Variable 1: 4) STRATIFIED
       Variable 2: 6) POLITICIAN

STRATIFIED -- DEGREE OF SOCIAL STRATIFICATION (M&P)

r = 0.465**

Exercise 6: Stratification

POLITICIAN -- DO FULL-TIME POLITICAL SPECIALISTS EXIST? (R)

A major cause of increased stratification is that as societies become more complex and wealthier, they begin to be run by specialists. That is, some people devote full-time to "politics"—to being in charge. Out of this emerges the **state**—an organized structure of leadership and control that attempts to monopolize the use of force within a society. Those who control the state are very powerful, and when people become very powerful, they will tend to use their power for their own benefit.

COMPARING MAPS:
  Variable 1: 4) STRATIFIED
  Variable 2: 5) STATE?

STRATIFIED -- DEGREE OF SOCIAL STRATIFICATION (M&P)

r = 0.660**

STATE? -- SCOPE OF POLITICAL INSTITUTIONS: STATELESS TO STATE (M&P)

The state offers many benefits. Typically the state is able to preserve internal order and to protect the society from external threats. But, as noted, the price of giving some people the power to run a society is that they inevitably tend to use their power for their own benefit. Thus, societies having states tend to be more stratified than stateless societies.

MAPPING: 41) $ RICH 10%

$ RICH 10% -- PERCENTAGE OF NATIONAL INCOME RECEIVED BY THE RICHEST 10 PERCENT (WDR)

This is a widely used cross-national measure of the degree of stratification: how much of all wealth goes to the richest 10 percent of the population. Keep in mind that this always will be *more* than 10 percent; otherwise, the society would be unstratified.

LIST RANK

RANK	CASE NAME	VALUE
1	Zimbabwe	55.5
2	Swaziland	54.5
3	Gabon	54.4
4	Ecuador	51.5
5	Nepal	50.7
6	Honduras	50.6
7	Brazil	48.3
8	Mauritius	46.4
9	Zambia	46.4
10	Kenya	45.8

Zimbabwe (55.5 percent) and Swaziland (54.5 percent) are the most stratified of these nations. Their rates indicate that the richest 10 percent of people in these two nations receive more than half of all wealth. Mexico (40.6 percent) is toward the middle; Canada (30.1 percent) is more stratified than the United States (28.2 percent) and Hungary (20.5 percent) is the least stratified.

Your turn.

Exercise 7:
Intergroup Relations

TASKS: Mapping, Correlation, Univariate, Cross-Tabulation
DATA FILES: GLOBAL, STATES, COUNTIES, SURVEY

Inaccurate negative beliefs and hostile feelings about a group are identified as **prejudice**. These are not beliefs and feelings about an individual but, rather, about a group. For example, it is not prejudice to think George is dishonest, even if this is not true. It becomes prejudice when we conclude that George must be dishonest because he is a Bluedonian, and "it is well-known" that all Bluedonians are thieves and liars. Harmful actions done to members of a group merely because they belong to that group are referred to as **discrimination**.

Conflicts between racial, religious, ethnic, and cultural groups have existed throughout history and occur around the world. All noticeable racial and cultural differences can arouse prejudice and lead to discrimination.

OPEN FILE: GLOBAL

MAPPING: 55) RACISM

RACISM -- PERCENT WHO WOULD NOT WANT MEMBERS OF ANOTHER RACE AS NEIGHBORS (WVS)

The recent World Values Surveys asked people in many nations a set of questions about whom they would be willing to have as neighbors. Here we see a map of the percentages who would not want neighbors of another race.

RANK	CASE NAME	VALUE
1	South Korea	58
2	Bulgaria	39
3	India	36
4	Turkey	32
5	Romania	30
6	Mexico	27
7	Macedonia	26
8	Finland	25
8	Bosnia	25
10	Nigeria	24

Look carefully at the top twelve most "racist" nations. Four of them are Asian: South Korea (58%), India (36%), Philippines (24%), and China (23%). Nigeria (24%) is in Africa and Turkey (32%) is in the Middle East. Four are in the Balkans: Bulgaria (39%), Romania (30%), Macedonia (26%), and Bosnia (25%). Finland (25%) is the only Western European nation among them, and Mexico (27%) is the only one in the Western Hemisphere.

In contrast, the least "racist" nations are in Western Europe and North and South America.

MAPPING: 54) ANTI-FORGN

ANTI-FORGN -- PERCENT WHO WOULD NOT WANT FOREIGNERS AS NEIGHBORS (WVS)

Turning from the issue of race to that of "ethnicity," this map shows the percentages who would not want foreigners as neighbors.

LIST RANK

RANK	CASE NAME	VALUE
1	South Korea	39
2	Turkey	36
3	India	33
3	Romania	33
5	Bangladesh	30
5	Lithuania	30
7	Czech Republic	28
8	Mexico	27
9	Taiwan	25
9	Hungary	25

Again South Korea (39 percent) is at the top of the list, closely followed by Turkey (36 percent), India (33 percent), Romania (33 percent), then Bangladesh and Lithuania at 30 percent.

MAPPING: 57) ANTI-SEM

ANTI-SEM. -- PERCENT WHO WOULD NOT WANT JEWS AS NEIGHBORS (WVS)

Prejudice and discrimination against Jews is known as anti-Semitism. Here the fundamental "difference" concerns religion. This map shows the percentages who would not want "Jews" as neighbors.

LIST RANK

RANK	CASE NAME	VALUE
1	India	86
2	Turkey	59
3	Slovenia	37
4	Nigeria	34
5	Bulgaria	30
6	Japan	28
6	Romania	28
8	Slovak Republic	27
9	Belarus	21
10	Portugal	19

India (86 percent) and Turkey (59 percent) are the most anti-Semitic nations, followed by Slovenia (37 percent), Nigeria (34 percent), Bulgaria (30 percent), and Japan (28 percent).

MAPPING: 58) ANTI-GAY

ANTI-GAY – PERCENT WHO WOULD NOT WANT HOMOSEXUALS AS NEIGHBORS (WVS)

Finally, we may consider a purely "cultural" difference. This map shows the percentages who would not want homosexuals as neighbors.

RANK	CASE NAME	VALUE
1	Azerbaijan	91
2	Nigeria	89
2	Turkey	89
4	Bangladesh	84
5	Armenia	83
6	Moldova	77
6	Lithuania	77
6	Georgia	77
9	Serbia	74
10	Russia	71

Citizens of Azerbaijan (91 percent) are most opposed to having homosexual neighbors, with Nigerians and Turks tied for second place (89 percent). In fact, there is far greater opposition to homosexual neighbors than to foreigners, Jews, or members of another race. In the United States and Canada, 30 percent object.

These variables measure prejudice and the willingness to discriminate. But they tell us very little about the actual cultural diversity of nations.

MAPPING: 43) MULTI-CULT

MULTI-CULT -- MULTI-CULTURALISM:ODDS THAT ANY 2 PERSONS WILL DIFFER IN THEIR RACE, RELIGION, ETHNICITY (TRIBE),OR LANGUAGE GROUP (STARK)

This map shows the multiculturalism (or diversity) index score for nations. It is based on a complex calculation of the odds that any two persons selected at random within a country would differ in terms of their race, religion, ethnicity (tribe), or language group. The higher the score, the higher the odds that pairs would differ.

LIST RANK

RANK	CASE NAME	VALUE
1	India	91
1	Congo, Dem Republic	91
3	Bolivia	90
4	Uganda	89
4	Camaroon	89
6	Nigeria	88
7	South Africa	87
8	Cote d'Ivoire	86
9	Bhutan	85
9	Congo Republic	85

Doing Sociology

India and the Democratic Republic of the Congo have the highest multiculturalism scores (91). That means that if 100 pairs of persons were randomly selected in each nation, 91 of the selected pairs would differ culturally. Canada is in 24th place (75) and the United States (63) is 58th. In Haiti, Portugal, and Japan, only one pair out of 100 would differ and in North Korea all pairs would be the same.

MAPPING: 44) C.CONFLICT
CLICK ON: Legend

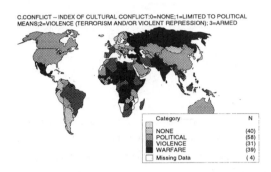

This map shows the levels of cultural conflict found around the world. Four levels are identified. Highest (3) is armed conflict or warfare. Altogether 39 nations were scored 3. Next highest (2) is violence, the existence of terrorism and/or violent repression, falling short of sustained warfare. A total of 31 nations were given his score. In an additional 58, cultural conflicts are confined to political means. And in 40 nations there was no significant conflict taking place.

OPEN FILE: STATES

MAPPING: 42) DIVERSITY

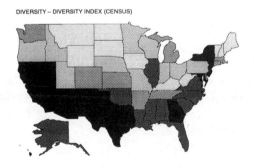

Following the U.S. Census conducted in 2000, statisticians at the Bureau of the Census calculated a diversity index for various geographic units. It is based on the same logic as the one shown above for nations: the odds that random pairs will be different. However, only basic racial and ethnic identities were considered: percent white; percent African American; percent Hispanic; percent Asian; percent Pacific Islander; and percent American Indian.

RANK	CASE NAME	VALUE
1	California	68.9
2	New Mexico	66.1
3	Hawaii	64.0
4	Texas	62.4
5	New York	57.6
6	Arizona	54.2
7	Nevada	53.7
8	Maryland	53.3
9	New Jersey	52.6
10	Georgia	52.2

Diversity tends to be a coastal phenomenon: highest along the Pacific, Gulf, and Atlantic Coasts. California is highest in terms of diversity. There, of every 100 pairs randomly selected, 68.9 would differ. New Mexico (66.1) is a very close second, followed by Hawaii (64.0), Texas (62.4), and New York (57.6). New Hampshire (9.7), Vermont (7.6), and Maine (6.9) are the least diverse states.

OPEN FILE: COUNTIES

MAPPING: 12) DIVERSITY

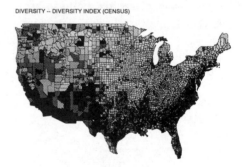

DIVERSITY -- DIVERSITY INDEX (CENSUS)

This map shows diversity for the more than 3,000 American counties. While it offers far greater detail than the state map, it too shows that diversity tends to be bicoastal.

LIST RANK

RANK	CASE NAME	VALUE
1	Kalawao, HI	87.9
2	Bronx, NY	80.7
3	Hawaii, HI	79.5
4	Queens, NY	76.3
5	Los Angeles, CA	76.2
6	Cibola, NM	75.2
7	Hudson, NJ	74.9
8	Kings, NY	73.5
9	Maui, HI	73.0
10	New York, NY	71.9

Of the five most diverse counties, two are in Hawaii, two are in New York City (Bronx and Queens), and one is Los Angeles.

OPEN FILE: SURVEY

Respondents in this national survey were asked a series of questions about how they would react if a close relative of theirs were to marry a person belonging to various racial, ethnic, and religious groups. This is a very "stringent" test of prejudice in that lots of people who have no qualms about having various groups for neighbors or classmates, balk at having them become part of their family.

UNIVARIATE: 48) MARRY A-AM

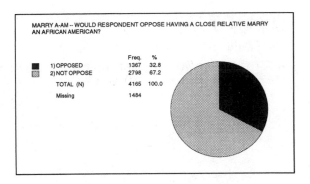

Here we see that a third of Americans would oppose having a close relative marry an African American.

UNIVARIATE: 49) MARRY HISP

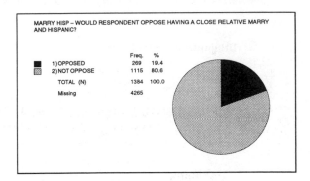

There is less opposition to marriage involving a Hispanic, but still one out of five would oppose it.

UNIVARIATE: 50) MARRY ASIA

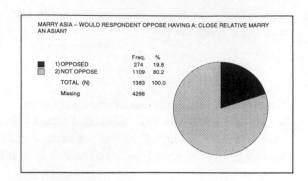

Opposition to intermarriage with an Asian is the same as for a Hispanic.

UNIVARIATE: 51) MARRY JEW

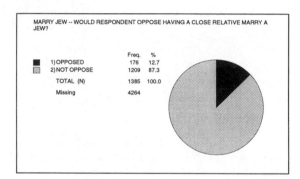

Opposition is even lower (12.7 percent) to having a relative marry a Jew.

UNIVARIATE: 52) MARRY WHIT

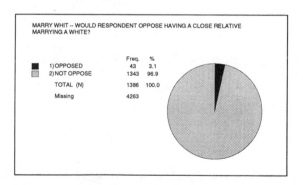

Finally, 3 percent would be opposed to having a relative marry a white.

Your turn.

WORKSHEET

NAME: _____

COURSE: _____

DATE: _____

EXERCISE

7

REVIEW QUESTIONS

Based on the first part of this exercise, answer True or False to the following items:

Nations having mainly nonwhite populations tend to have very few racists.	T F
Japan scores very high on diversity.	T F
The diversity index for states and counties based on the 2000 U.S. Census gives particular weight to religious differences.	T F
Americans are much more willing to have a relative marry an Asian than they are to have them marry a Hispanic.	T F
Refusal to marry someone because of their race is an example of prejudice.	T F

OPEN FILE: GLOBAL

1. **Hypothesis:** *All valid measures of prejudice will be highly correlated.*

    CORRELATION:
    SELECT VARIABLES: 55) RACISM
    54) ANTI-FORGN
    57) ANTI-SEM.
    11) TV SETS
    58) ANTI-GAY
    43) MULTI-CULT
    42) INEQUALITY

    On the basis of correlations alone, which of these variables should not be considered as a measure of prejudice?

    List: _____

    _____

    On the basis of reason and logic, are there any variables that should not be considered as a measure of prejudice?

    List: _____

    _____

Exercise 7: Intergroup Relations

107

Explain your selection(s):

_____

_____

_____

_____

2. **Hypothesis:** *The more modernized a nation, the fewer people who will be prejudiced.*

    CORRELATION:
    SELECT VARIABLES: 3) $ GDP/CAP
                           55) RACISM
                           54) ANTI-FORGN
                           57) ANTI-SEM.
                           58) ANTI-GAY

    What is the value of the correlation coefficient between $ GDP/CAP and each of these measures of prejudice?

    RACISM   _____

    ANTI-FORGN   _____

    ANTI-SEM.   _____

    ANTI-GAY   _____

    How many of these correlations are negative? (Circle one.)   0   1   2   3   4

    How many are statistically significant? (Circle one.)   0   1   2   3   4

    How many support the hypothesis? (Circle one.)   0   1   2   3   4

3. **Hypothesis:** *The higher the percentage of Christians in a nation, the more people who will be prejudiced.*

    CORRELATION:
    SELECT VARIABLES: 37) %CHRISTIAN
                           55) RACISM
                           54) ANTI-FORGN
                           57) ANTI-SEM.
                           58) ANTI-GAY

What is the value of the correlation coefficient between %CHRISTIAN and each of these measures of prejudice?

RACISM   _____

ANTI-FORGN   _____

ANTI-SEM.   _____

ANTI-GAY   _____

How many of these correlations are negative? (Circle one.)   0   1   2   3   4

How many are statistically significant? (Circle one.)   0   1   2   3   4

How many support the hypothesis? (Circle one.)   0   1   2   3   4

4.   **Hypothesis:** *The higher the percentage of Muslims in a nation, the more people who will be prejudiced.*

    CORRELATION:

SELECT VARIABLES: 38) %MUSLIM
                      55) RACISM
                      54) ANTI-FORGN
                      57) ANTI-SEM.
                      58) ANTI-GAY

What is the value of the correlation coefficient between %MUSLIM and each of these measures of prejudice?

RACISM   _____

ANTI-FORGN   _____

ANTI-SEM.   _____

ANTI-GAY   _____

How many of these correlations are negative? (Circle one.)   0   1   2   3   4

How many are statistically significant? (Circle one.)   0   1   2   3   4

How many support the hypothesis? (Circle one.)   0   1   2   3   4

    OPEN FILE: COUNTIES

    MAPPING: 15) % A.INDIAN

Looking back at the map of sampling points for the General Social Surveys, shown in Exercise 2, would you expect American Indians to be over- or under-represented in the SURVEY data file? (Circle one.)   Over   Under

MAPPING: 10) %P.ISLANDER

Looking back at the map of sampling points for the General Social Surveys, shown in Exercise 2, would you expect Pacific Islanders to be over- or under-represented in the SURVEY data file? (Circle one.)   Over   Under

OPEN FILE: SURVEY

5. **Hypothesis:** *Anglo whites will be the group most likely to oppose intermarriage with an African American.*

CROSS-TABULATION:
      ROW VARIABLE: 48) MARRY A-AM
COLUMN VARIABLE 2: 4) RACE/ETHNI
            COLUMN %

In which group is the percentage opposed highest?   _____

In which group is the percentage opposed lowest?   _____

What is the value of V for this table?   V = _____

Is it negative or positive?   Negative   Positive

Is V statistically significant?   Yes   No

Is the hypothesis supported or rejected?   Supported   Rejected

6. **Hypothesis:** *Anglo whites will be the group most likely to oppose intermarriage with a Jew.*

CROSS-TABULATION:
      ROW VARIABLE: 51) MARRY JEW
COLUMN VARIABLE 2: 4) RACE/ETHNI
            COLUMN %

In which group is the percentage opposed highest?   _____

In which group is the percentage opposed lowest?   _____

What is the value of V for this table?   V = _____

Is it negative or positive?   Negative   Positive

Is V statistically significant?   Yes   No

Is the hypothesis supported or rejected?   Supported   Rejected

7. **Hypothesis:** *African Americans will be the group most likely to oppose intermarriage with a white.*

CROSS-TABULATION:
    ROW VARIABLE: 52) MARRY WHIT
COLUMN VARIABLE 2: 4) RACE/ETHNI
        COLUMN %

In which group is the percentage opposed highest?   _____

In which group is the percentage opposed lowest?   _____

What is the value of V for this table?   V = _____

Is it negative or positive?   Negative   Positive

Is V statistically significant?   Yes   No

Is the hypothesis supported or rejected?   Supported   Rejected

8. **Hypothesis:** *People with higher incomes will be the group most likely to oppose intermarriage with an African American.*

CROSS-TABULATION:
    ROW VARIABLE: 48) MARRY A-AM
COLUMN VARIABLE 2: 11) $ –50/+50K
        COLUMN %

In which group is the percentage opposed highest?   _____

What is the value of V for this table?   V = _____

Is it negative or positive?   Negative   Positive

Is V statistically significant?   Yes   No

Is the hypothesis supported or rejected?   Supported   Rejected

9.   **Hypothesis:** *The older they are, the more likely people are to oppose intermarriage with an African American.*

CROSS-TABULATION:
   ROW VARIABLE: 48) MARRY A-AM
COLUMN VARIABLE 2: 6) AGE
         COLUMN %

In which group is the percentage opposed highest?   _____

In which group is the percentage opposed lowest?   _____

What is the value of V for this table?   V = _____

Is it negative or positive?   Negative   Positive

Is V statistically significant?   Yes   No

Is the hypothesis supported or rejected?   Supported   Rejected

A sociologist who looked at this table said, "That's great! We are making real progress." What do you suppose this sociologist was talking about?

_____

_____

_____

_____

_____

_____

_____

_____

_____

10. Reflecting on all of the findings in this exercise, what was the single most important thing you think you learned?

_____

_____

_____

_____

_____

_____

_____

_____

_____

_____

_____

_____

_____

_____

EXERCISE 8:
MARITAL SATISFACTION

TASKS: Mapping, Univariate, Cross-tabulation
DATA FILES: GLOBAL, STATES, SURVEY

It would be hard to discover just how many books and articles have been written about the "decline" of marriage and the family in modern times—this has been one of the standard topics for at least a century. Rising divorce rates, a growing number of infants born out of wedlock, unmarried couples who live together—all are seen as symptoms of crisis and collapse proving that the family just isn't what it used to be. But is it true? Is marriage really on the way out? Were couples happier in more traditional families? Is life in modern, urban societies fundamentally incompatible with happy and lasting marriages?

In this exercise you will explore these issues.

OPEN FILE: GLOBAL

Let's start with the idea that marriage is on its way out, that one day soon couples no longer will bother having a legal or religious ceremony or making vows of life-long commitment. Instead, people will move in together, or not, as they please and there will be little expectation that relationships will be lasting. Predictions such as these inspired those who draft the World Values Surveys to discover what people in many nations think about this.

MAPPING: 49) WED PASSE'

WED PASSE' -- PERCENT WHO AGREE THAT "MARRIAGE IS AN OUTDATED INSTITUTION." (WVS)

This map shows variations in the percentage who agreed that "marriage is an outdated institution."

LIST RANK

RANK	CASE NAME	VALUE
1	Venezuela	31
2	France	29
2	Brazil	29
2	Moldova	29
5	Germany	28
6	Slovenia	25
6	Colombia	25
8	Switzerland	24
8	Mexico	24
10	India	23

This statement was rejected overwhelmingly in all of the surveyed nations. Agreement was highest in Venezuela (31 percent), France (29 percent), and Brazil (29 percent). In Canada only 12 percent agreed, as did 11 percent in the United States.

MAPPING: 59) HOME LIFE?

HOME LIFE? -- PERCENT WHO SAID THEY WERE "VERY SATISFIED" WITH THEIR HOME LIFE (WVS)

This map shows variations in the percentage who are "very satisfied" with their home life.

LIST RANK

RANK	CASE NAME	VALUE
1	Poland	65
2	Denmark	64
3	Switzerland	61
3	Ireland	61
5	Chile	58
6	United States	57
7	Canada	56
8	Brazil	55
8	Sweden	55
10	Finland	52

Here there is much variation. In Poland 65 percent are very satisfied, but in Japan only 17 percent and only 12 percent in Estonia are very satisfied.

Any well-stocked magazine rack includes dozens of articles about how to have a happy marriage. Nearly all of these focus on the fundamental aspect of marriage as relationship: symmetry. The idea is that both partners will benefit equally from the relationship as each contributes equally. Marriages

Doing Sociology

will be happy to the extent that both partners love one another and each fully contributes to demands of everyday life.

Let's explore the validity of these two claims.

Hypothesis: *People will be more satisfied with their home lives in nations where they also are more satisfied with their sex lives.*

COMPARING MAPS:
      Variable 1: 59) HOME LIFE?
      Variable 2: 60) HAPPY SEX?

HOME LIFE? -- PERCENT WHO SAID THEY WERE "VERY SATISFIED" WITH THEIR HOME LIFE (WVS)

r = 0.488**

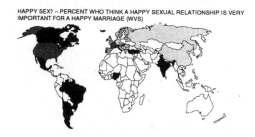

HAPPY SEX? -- PERCENT WHO THINK A HAPPY SEXUAL RELATIONSHIP IS VERY IMPORTANT FOR A HAPPY MARRIAGE (WVS)

This hypothesis is supported. A happy sex life does seem to make for a happy home life.

Hypothesis: *People will be more satisfied with their home lives in nations where they also are more willing to share household chores.*

COMPARING MAPS:
      Variable 1: 59) HOME LIFE?
      Variable 2: 61) CHORES?

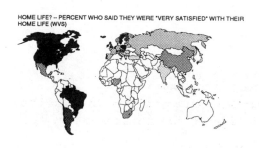

HOME LIFE? -- PERCENT WHO SAID THEY WERE "VERY SATISFIED" WITH THEIR HOME LIFE (WVS)

r = 0.431**

CHORES? -- PERCENT WHO THINK THAT "SHARING HOUSEHOLD CHORES" IS "VERY IMPORTANT" TO A HAPPY MARRIAGE (WVS)

Sharing household chores also makes for a happy home life. It appears that the magazines know something.

Hypothesis: *People will be more satisfied with their home lives in nations where people hold a traditional view of marriage and motherhood.*

COMPARING MAPS:
      Variable 1: 59) HOME LIFE?
      Variable 2: 47) SINGLE MOM

HOME LIFE? -- PERCENT WHO SAID THEY WERE "VERY SATISFIED" WITH THEIR HOME LIFE (WVS)

r = −0.034

SINGLE MOM -- PERCENT WHO APPROVE OF A WOMAN CHOOSING TO BE A SINGLE PARENT (WVS)

Wrong! There is no correlation.

Hypothesis: *People will be more satisfied with their home lives in less economically developed nations.*

Doing Sociology

COMPARING MAPS:
      Variable 1: 59) HOME LIFE?
      Variable 2: 50) ECON DEVEL

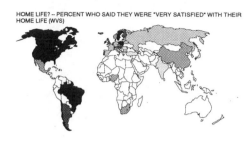

HOME LIFE? -- PERCENT WHO SAID THEY WERE "VERY SATISFIED" WITH THEIR HOME LIFE (WVS)

r = 0.035

ECON DEVEL -- LEVEL OF ECONOMIC DEVELOPMENT (HDR)

Wrong again! Economic development is unrelated to satisfaction.

OPEN FILE: STATES

There are no surveys including enough cases so that we can characterize states in terms of the percentages who are very satisfied with their home lives or who say that their marriages are very happy. But is seems reasonable to interpret divorce statistics this way. That is, if a larger proportion of a state's population is divorced, one may suppose that this was in response to a larger proportion of unsatisfactory marriages.

MAPPING: 20) %DIVORCED

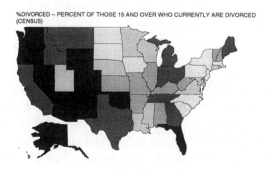

%DIVORCED -- PERCENT OF THOSE 15 AND OVER WHO CURRENTLY ARE DIVORCED (CENSUS)

There is a very clear geography of divorce—it is very western.

RANK	CASE NAME	VALUE
1	Nevada	14.4
2	Alaska	11.1
3	Oregon	10.8
4	Colorado	10.7
5	Washington	10.6
6	Arizona	10.3
7	New Mexico	10.2
8	Florida	10.1
8	Oklahoma	10.1
10	Wyoming	9.9

Nevada has the highest percentage of divorced residents, followed by Alaska, Oregon, Colorado, and Washington. North Dakota is the lowest state, but New Jersey and New York are the next lowest.

COMPARING MAPS:
  Variable 1: 20) %DIVORCED
  Variable 2: 45) MARRY RATE

%DIVORCED -- PERCENT OF THOSE 15 AND OVER WHO CURRENTLY ARE DIVORCED (CENSUS)

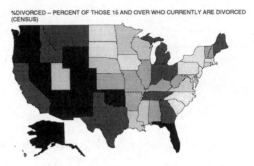

r = 0.573**

MARRY RATE -- MARRIAGES PER 1,000 POPULATION (S.A)

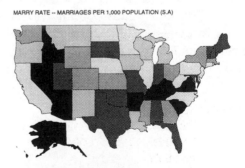

States with the highest percentage of divorced people also have the highest marriage rates. There are two reasons for this. First of all, only married people can get divorced so it requires a lot of marriages in order to have a lot of divorces. Second, the more often people get divorced, the more often they can get married. This is sometimes called the "Liz Taylor effect." A couple who marry once and never divorce contribute to the marriage rate of their home state only once—in the year they were wed. But people who frequently divorce contribute to the marriage rate again and again.

OPEN FILE: SURVEY

UNIVARIATE: 53) BEEN DIVOR

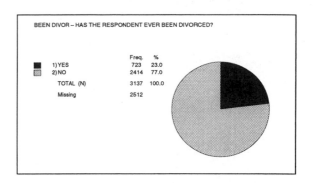

Among Americans 18 and older, about 2 in 10, have been divorced at least once. Of course, some of those who had not yet been divorced when they were interviewed eventually will do so, which means that the "final" figure will be higher than this. This could mean that a large percentage of American marriages are unhappy. But it also could mean that people generally terminate unhappy marriages and therefore that at any given moment, most marriages are quite happy. Let's see.

UNIVARIATE: 22) HAPPY MAR?

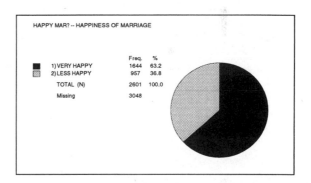

In fact, 6 of 10 married Americans rate their marriage as "Very happy." Some suggest that people who have ended an unhappy marriage do better the next time around. Others suggest that people who get divorced tend to have flaws that show up the next time around too.

CROSS-TABULATION:
Row Variable: 22) HAPPY MAR?
Column Variable: 53) BEEN DIVOR
Column%

HAPPY MAR?   by   BEEN DIVOR
Cramer's V: 0.005

		BEEN DIVOR			
		YES	NO	Missing	TOTAL
HAPPY MAR?	VERY HAPPY	382	1247	15	1629
		62.7%	63.3%		63.1%
	LESS HAPPY	227	724	6	951
		37.3%	36.7%		36.9%
	Missing	114	443	2491	3048
	TOTAL	609	1971	2512	2580
		100.0%	100.0%		

To the extent that this is an adequate test, both expectations are incorrect. People who have been divorced do not differ from those who have not in terms of their marital happiness.

Your turn.

Exercise 8: Marital Satisfaction

WORKSHEET

NAME:

COURSE:

DATE:

REVIEW QUESTIONS

Based on the first part of this exercise, answer True or False to the following items:

In northern European nations such as Sweden and Denmark, more than half of the population believe marriage is "outdated."	T F
Most Japanese are very satisfied with their home lives.	T F
In general, people are more satisfied with their home lives in more traditional societies.	T F
High divorce rates are associated with high marriage rates.	T F
People who are remarried have less happy marriages than do people in their first marriage.	T F

OPEN FILE: SURVEY

1. **Hypothesis:** *People who have been unfaithful are more likely to have been divorced.*

CROSS-TABULATION:
 ROW VARIABLE: 53) BEEN DIVOR
 COLUMN VARIABLE: 21) UNFAITHFUL
 Column %

Copy the first row of the percentaged table:

21) UNFAITHFUL

	CHEATED	FAITHFUL
DIVORCED	_____%	_____%

Which group is most apt to have been divorced? _____

What is the value of V for this table? V = _____

Is V statistically significant? Yes   No

Is the hypothesis supported or rejected? Supported   Rejected

2. **Hypothesis:** *People who have been faithful will have happier current marriages.*

CROSS-TABULATION:
      ROW VARIABLE: 22) HAPPY MAR?
  COLUMN VARIABLE: 21) UNFAITHFUL
        Column %

Copy the first row of the percentaged table:

21) UNFAITHFUL	CHEATED	FAITHFUL
VERY HAPPY	_____%	_____%

Which group is most apt to be very happy in their marriage?   _____

What is the value of V for this table?   V = _____

Is V statistically significant?   Yes   No

Is the hypothesis supported or rejected?   Supported   Rejected

3. **Hypothesis:** *The more often people have sex, the happier their marriage.*

CROSS-TABULATION:
      ROW VARIABLE: 22) HAPPY MAR?
  COLUMN VARIABLE: 23) SEX OFTEN?
        Column %

Copy the first row of the percentaged table:

23) SEX OFTEN?	RARE/NEVER	MONTHLY	WEEKLY
VERY HAPPY	_____%	_____%	_____%

Which group is most apt to be very happy in their marriage?   _____

What is the value of V for this table?   V = _____

Is V statistically significant?   Yes   No

Is the hypothesis supported or rejected?   Supported   Rejected

On the basis of this table, answer True or False to the following questions:

Most couples who never have sex, or do so only rarely, are not very happy.   T   F

It could be argued that it isn't sex that makes people happy, but that happy couples
tend to have frequent sex.   T   F

This finding contradicts the one found with the GLOBAL data set.   T   F

4.   **Hypothesis:** *The more often people go to bars, the less happy their marriage.*

CROSS-TABULATION:
       ROW VARIABLE: 22) HAPPY MAR?
COLUMN VARIABLE: 46) GO 2 BARS
              Column %

Copy the first row of the percentaged table:

46) GO 2 BARS

	WEEKLY +	1–2 MONTH	SOMETIMES	NEVER
VERY HAPPY	_____%	_____%	_____%	_____%

Which group is most apt to be very happy in their marriage?   _____

Which group is least apt to be very happy?   _____

What is the value of V for this table?   V = _____

Is V statistically significant?   Yes   No

Is the hypothesis supported or rejected?   Supported   Rejected

5.   **Hypothesis:** *People with higher family incomes will tend to have happier marriages.*

CROSS-TABULATION:
       ROW VARIABLE: 22) HAPPY MAR?
COLUMN VARIABLE: 10) FAMILY $
              Column %

Copy the first row of the percentaged table:

10) FAMILY $

	UNDER 15K	$15–$29K	$30–$49K	$50K$90K	OVER $90K
VERY HAPPY	_____%	_____%	_____%	_____%	_____%

Which group is most apt to be very happy in their marriage?   _____

Which group is least apt to be very happy?   _____

What is the value of V for this table?   V = _____

Is V statistically significant?   Yes   No

Is the hypothesis supported or rejected?   Supported   Rejected

6. **Hypothesis:** *The more often people go to church, the less happy their marriage.*

CROSS-TABULATION:
    ROW VARIABLE: 22) HAPPY MAR?
  COLUMN VARIABLE: 13) CH.ATTEND
        Column %

Copy the first row of the percentaged table:

13) CH.ATTEND

	WEEKLY	MONTHLY	1–2 YEAR	RARE/NEVER
VERY HAPPY	_____%	_____%	_____%	_____%

Which group is most apt to be very happy in their marriage?   _____

Which group is least apt to be very happy?   _____

What is the value of V for this table?   V = _____

Is V statistically significant?   Yes   No

Is the hypothesis supported or rejected?   Supported   Rejected

On the basis of these results, formulate and test this hypothesis:

> **OPEN FILE:** STATES

7. **Hypothesis:** *Divorce will be (select one)* ❑ *higher* ❑ *lower in states where more people are church members.*

COMPARING MAPS:
> **VARIABLE 1:** 20) %DIVORCED
> **VARIABLE 2:** 14) CH.MEMBERS

What is the value of r?   r = _____

Is it negative or positive?   Negative   Positive

Is it significant?   Yes   No

Is the hypothesis supported or rejected?   Supported   Rejected

8. Summarize these findings and those in the front section to answer the question: What contributes to a happy marriage?

_____

_____

_____

_____

_____

_____

_____

_____

_____

_____

_____

_____

_____

Exercise 8: Marital Satisfaction

EXERCISE 9:
RELIGION

TASKS: Mapping, Univariate, Cross-tabulation
DATA FILES: STATES, COUNTIES, SURVEY

For more than three centuries, Western intellectuals have been predicting the end of religion. In one paragraph of his famous book *Leviathan* (written in the 1640s), the English social philosopher Thomas Hobbes dismissed all religion as "credulity," "ignorance," and "lies," and fated to disappear as humans became educated. Another Englishman, Thomas Woolston, was the first to set a date by which the end of religion would be achieved, writing in 1710 that religious beliefs would be only a memory by 1900. Half a century later, Frederick the Great, ruler of Prussia and part-time intellectual, wrote to his friend Voltaire that Woolston was wrong, that the end of religion would come much sooner. The famous French philosopher agreed with Frederick, responding that it would be all over within 50 years.

The belief that religion is doomed to die out in the modern world is known as the **secularization theory** (*secular* refers to worldly things as distinguished from religious or otherworldly things). For a very long time the secularization theory was almost universally accepted and taught by social scientists. Had you taken a sociology course even 20 years ago your text probably would have presented secularization as a process well-underway and the secularization theory as one of the major achievements of the field. Your book might even have quoted Peter Berger's colorful formulation which appeared in the *New York Times* (4/25/68:3) that by "the 21st century, religious believers are likely to be found only in small sects, huddled together to resist a worldwide secular culture. . . . The predicament of the believer is increasingly like that of a Tibetan astrologer on a prolonged visit to an American university."

In light of the recent welcome given to the Dalai Lama on many American campuses, Berger's simile now seems less than apt. In any event, when his prediction had only three years left to run, Berger gracefully took it back, admitting that he, and most other social scientists, had been completely wrong. As Berger acknowledged, religion is as strong as ever—stronger in many places.

So, in this exercise we will explore religion and pursue some rather surprising aspects that may help explain why the secularization thesis was wrong.

OPEN FILE: STATES

MAPPING: 15) % NO RELIG

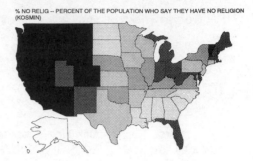

This map is based on a huge survey of 113,000 Americans, all of whom were asked their religious preference. Here is the percentage in each state who said they had "no religion." Hawaii and Alaska were not included in the survey. Notice that lack of a religion is very western.

LIST RANK

RANK	CASE NAME	VALUE
1	Oregon	17.2
2	Washington	14.0
3	Wyoming	13.5
4	Nevada	13.2
5	California	13.0
6	Arizona	12.2
7	Idaho	11.9
8	Vermont	11.4
8	Colorado	11.4
10	Montana	10.2

Although they are more prevalent in the West, people with "no religion" are not so numerous anywhere. They are easiest to find in Oregon where 17.2 percent said they had "no religion." Next highest is Washington, then comes Wyoming. In contrast, only 2.5 percent in South Dakota and 1.6 percent in North Dakota said, "no religion."

It is widely believed that the American South is the "Bible Belt." But notice that the South does not differ from the Midwest and East on this measure.

MAPPING: 14) CH.MEMBERS

CH.MEMBERS -- PERCENT OF POPULATION BELONGING TO A LOCAL CHURCH (CHURCH)

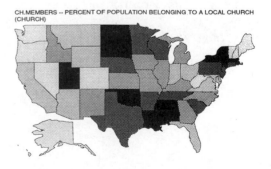

Doing Sociology

Nor does the South stand out on the percent, who belong to a local church (as opposed simply to stating a religious preference). As we will see, about 90 percent of Americans state a preference, but about a third of them do not have an active membership locally.

LIST RANK

RANK	CASE NAME	VALUE
1	Utah	79.8
2	Rhode Island	76.7
3	North Dakota	75.9
4	Alabama	71.0
5	Louisiana	70.5
6	Mississippi	70.2
7	South Dakota	68.1
8	Oklahoma	66.8
9	New York	65.7
10	Massachusetts	65.5

Utah has the highest percentage of church members, followed by Rhode Island and North Dakota. And once again it is the West that differs from the rest of the nation—Alaska having the lowest church membership rate, followed by Oregon and Nevada. Thus, while it is impossible to spot a "Bible Belt" in terms of religious preference or church membership, there is an "Unchurched Belt" along the West Coast.

MAPPING: 47) % BAPTIST

% BAPTIST -- PERCENT OF THE POPULATION WHO GIVE THEIR RELIGIOUS PREFERENCE AS BAPTIST (KOSMIN)

There is a Southern "Baptist Belt."

LIST RANK

RANK	CASE NAME	VALUE
1	Mississippi	55.0
2	Alabama	51.4
3	Georgia	50.8
4	North Carolina	47.1
5	South Carolina	46.5
6	Tennessee	43.0
7	Kentucky	42.5
8	Arkansas	42.2
9	Oklahoma	32.6
10	Texas	32.0

Mississippi is the most Baptist state, followed by Alabama and Georgia. Baptists are least common in Utah and Minnesota.

MAPPING: 48) % CATHOLIC

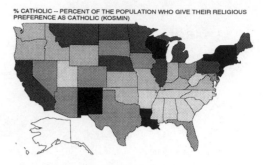

% CATHOLIC -- PERCENT OF THE POPULATION WHO GIVE THEIR RELIGIOUS PREFERENCE AS CATHOLIC (KOSMIN)

Catholics are almost the mirror image of Baptists, being highest in the Northeast and upper Midwest and lowest in the South (except for Louisiana where the French heritage is obvious).

LIST RANK

RANK	CASE NAME	VALUE
1	Rhode Island	61.7
2	Massachusetts	54.3
3	Connecticut	50.4
4	Louisiana	46.8
5	New Jersey	45.9
6	New York	44.3
7	New Hampshire	41.3
8	Wisconsin	38.6
9	New Mexico	37.3
10	Vermont	36.7

Rhode Island is the most Catholic state followed by Massachusetts and Connecticut. Catholics are least common in Alabama and Tennessee.

MAPPING: 16) % JEWISH

% JEWISH -- PERCENT OF THE POPULATION WHO GIVE THEIR RELIGIOUS PREFERENCES AS JEWISH (KOSMIN)

The Jewish population is very coastal, along the Atlantic, Gulf, and Pacific.

Doing Sociology

RANK	CASE NAME	VALUE
1	New York	6.9
2	New Jersey	4.3
3	Florida	3.6
4	Massachusetts	3.5
5	Maryland	2.8
6	Connecticut	2.4
7	California	2.3
8	Colorado	1.8
9	Pennsylvania	1.7
10	Rhode Island	1.6

New York has the highest percentage of Jews, but even so Jews make up only a small percentage of the population (6.9 percent). There are very few Jews living in the plains states or the South (except for Florida).

MAPPING: 44) CULTS

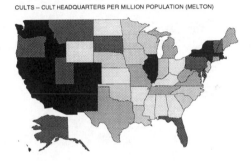

CULTS -- CULT HEADQUARTERS PER MILLION POPULATION (MELTON)

The news media often use the word *cult* to attack some small religious groups as evil, wicked, or crazy and its members as victims of deceitful leaders. That's not what it means to sociologists. For sociologists, cults are any and all religious groups that are outside the conventional religious tradition of the society in question. Thus, for example, Christianity is classified as a cult in India and Hinduism is classified as a cult in the United States. Put another way, a cult is simply a novel or unusual religious group.

This map is based on the location of the headquarters of all the known cults in the nation. Nearly all cults are very small and have only one unit, so they exist only where their headquarters is located. As can be seen, cults are more successful in the western parts of the United States.

LIST RANK

RANK	CASE NAME	VALUE
1	New Mexico	7.3
2	California	5.8
3	Nevada	4.2
4	New York	3.4
5	Colorado	3.3
5	Arizona	3.3
7	Massachusetts	2.7
7	Hawaii	2.7
9	Washington	2.5
10	Idaho	2.0

New Mexico has the highest rate, followed by California and Nevada. Wyoming, Kentucky, North Dakota, and Mississippi have no cult headquarters. Each probably has at least one cult center of one of the larger groups such as Scientology.

OPEN FILE: COUNTIES

MAPPING: 4) % JEWISH

% JEWISH -- PERCENT OF POPULATION WHO ARE JEWISH (CHURCH)

Now we see the Jewish population by counties. The highest density is in the large eastern cities, especially New York City. But, Florida and coastal California also display substantial Jewish populations.

MAPPING: 5) %CH. MEMBR

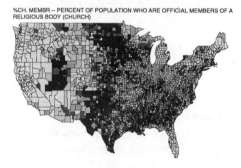

%CH. MEMBR -- PERCENT OF POPULATION WHO ARE OFFICIAL MEMBERS OF A RELIGIOUS BODY (CHURCH)

This map of church membership is similar to the map of church membership by states, but it has an unusual feature.

LIST RANK

RANK	CASE NAME	VALUE
1	Macon, AL	146.06
2	Roberts, TX	141.56
3	Winkler, TX	139.57
4	Hancock, TN	137.84
5	Rolette, ND	135.84
6	Ward, TX	133.46
7	Throckmorton, TX	128.03
8	Reeves, TX	127.47
9	Cottle, TX	125.10
10	Floyd, TX	124.30

Doing Sociology

Sixty-three counties have membership rates of more than 100 percent—Macon County, Alabama, has a rate of 146.06 percent. At the other extreme, some counties have no church members at all. What accounts for this is that the percent church members is calculated by dividing the number of members reported by the churches in each county by the total population. But some rural counties have no churches, and the people living in them belong to a church in the next county. That makes it possible for some counties to have more church members than residents, since the churches report all members including those who attend from another county.

The map shows the same concentration of church membership in the middle of the nation and on the East Coast revealed by the map for states.

OPEN FILE: SURVEY

Now let's explore American religion at the individual level.

UNIVARIATE: 14) REL CHOICE

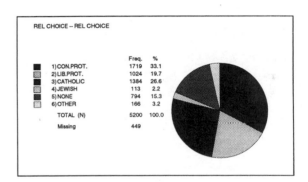

Here we see that most Americans claim a Protestant affiliation, and of these the majority are affiliated with a conservative denomination such as the Baptists. The Jewish population is small proportionately, even though more Jews live in the United States than in any other nation, including Israel. And only about 1 American in 10 identifies her or his religious preference as "None."

UNIVARIATE: 13) CH.ATTEND

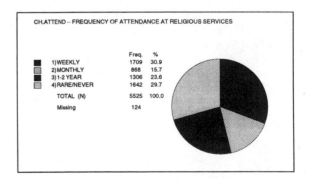

One American in 4 is a very frequent church attendee, going at least once a week (many go two or three times a week). About a third attend only rarely or never.

UNIVARIATE: 40) PRAYER?

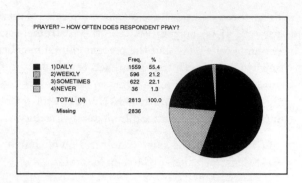

PRAYER? -- HOW OFTEN DOES RESPONDENT PRAY?

	Freq.	%
1) DAILY	1559	55.4
2) WEEKLY	596	21.2
3) SOMETIMES	622	22.1
4) NEVER	36	1.3
TOTAL (N)	2813	100.0
Missing	2836	

Americans pray a lot more than they attend church—most pray every day (many pray several times a day). Only about 1 in 50 never prays.

Your turn.

NAME:

COURSE:

DATE:

REVIEW QUESTIONS

Based on the first part of this exercise, answer True or False to the following items:

Secularization theory predicts the end of religion.	T	F
Church membership rates reveal that the South is a Bible Belt.	T	F
Jews are the largest religious group in New York State.	T	F
A cult is a religious group that harms its members.	T	F
About half of American adults pray less than once a week.	T	F

OPEN FILE: SURVEY

1. **Hypothesis:** *People who say they have no religion are the irreligious people to whom the secularization theory refers: they do not pray.*

CROSS-TABULATION:
  ROW VARIABLE: 40) PRAYER?
 COLUMN VARIABLE: 14) REL CHOICE
     Column %

Copy the fifth column of the percentaged table:

14) REL CHOICE

NONE

DAILY _____%

WEEKLY _____%

SOMETIMES _____%

NEVER _____%

Based on these results, evaluate and discuss this statement: Most Americans who give their religious affiliation as "none" do not mean "I am irreligious," but only "None of the above."

_____

_____

_____

_____

_____

_____

_____

_____

2. **Hypothesis:** *The secularization theory reasoned that education and religion were incompatible and religion therefore would disappear as more and more people became educated. It follows that the most highly educated will not attend church very often.*

CROSS-TABULATION:
     ROW VARIABLE: 13) CH.ATTEND
  COLUMN VARIABLE: 12) EDUCATION
           Column %

Copy the first row of the percentaged table:

12) EDUCATION

	NOT HS GRAD	HS GRAD	COLLEGE	GRAD SCHOOL
WEEKLY	_____%	_____%	_____%	_____%

What is the value of V for this table?   V = _____

Is V statistically significant?   Yes   No

Is the hypothesis supported or rejected?   Supported   Rejected

3. **Hypothesis:** *Women will tend to pray more often than men.*

CROSS-TABULATION:
    ROW VARIABLE: 40) PRAYER?
 COLUMN VARIABLE: 3) SEX
        Column %

Copy the first row of the percentaged table:

3) SEX	MALE	FEMALE
PRAY DAILY	_____%	_____%

Which group is most apt to pray daily?   _____

What is the value of V for this table?   V = _____

Is V statistically significant?   Yes   No

Is the hypothesis supported or rejected?   Supported   Rejected

4. **Hypothesis:** *Older people will tend to pray more often than younger people.*

CROSS-TABULATION:
    ROW VARIABLE: 40) PRAYER?
 COLUMN VARIABLE: 6) AGE
        Column %

Copy the first row of the percentaged table:

6) AGE	18–29	30–39	40–49	50–65	OVER 65
PRAY DAILY	_____%	_____%	_____%	_____%	_____%

What is the value of V for this table?   V = _____

Is V statistically significant?   Yes   No

Now copy the bottom row of the percentaged table:

6) AGE

	18–29	30–39	40–49	50–65	OVER 65
NEVER PRAY	_____%	_____%	_____%	_____%	_____%

Answer True or False to the following items:

The older they are, the more often people tend to pray.　　　　　　　　T　　F

Most people under 30 never pray.　　　　　　　　T　　F

5.　**Hypothesis:** *Older people tend to be less educated than younger people.*

CROSS-TABULATION:
　　ROW VARIABLE: 12) EDUCATION
　COLUMN VARIABLE: 6) AGE
　　　　Column %

Copy the first row of the percentaged table:

6) AGE

	18–29	30–39	40–49	50–65	OVER 65
-HIGH SCHOOL	_____%	_____%	_____%	_____%	_____%

What is the value of V for this table?　　　　　　　　V = _____

Is V statistically significant?　　　　　　　　Yes　　No

Is the hypothesis supported or rejected?　　　　　　　　Supported　　Rejected

6.　**Hypothesis:** *Among people under age 50, education will not be related to prayer.*

CROSS-TABULATION:
　　　ROW VARIABLE: 40) PRAYER?
　COLUMN VARIABLE: 12) EDUCATION
　SUBSET VARIABLE: 7) OVR/UND50
　　　CATEGORIES: 1) UNDER 50
　　　　Column %

Copy the first row of the percentaged table:

12) EDUCATION

	NOT HS GRAD	HS GRAD	COLLEGE	GRAD SCHOOL
PRAY DAILY	_____%	_____%	_____%	_____%

Which group is least apt to pray daily?   _____

Which group is the next lowest?   _____

What is the value of V for this table?   V = _____

Is V statistically significant?   Yes   No

Is the hypothesis supported or rejected?   Supported   Rejected

OPEN FILE: STATES

7.   **Hypothesis:** *Cult movements will cluster where more people say they have no religion.*

COMPARING MAPS:
     VARIABLE 1: 44) CULTS
     VARIABLE 2: 15) % NO RELIG

What is the value of r?   r = _____

Is it negative or positive?   Negative   Positive

Is it significant?   Yes   No

Is the hypothesis supported or rejected?   Supported   Rejected

8.   **Hypothesis:** *Professional astrologers will be clustered where more people say they have no religion.*

COMPARING MAPS:
     VARIABLE 1: 26) ASTROLOGER
     VARIABLE 2: 15) % NO RELIG

What is the value of r?   r = _____

Is it negative or positive?   Negative   Positive

Is it significant?   Yes   No

Is the hypothesis supported or rejected?   Supported   Rejected

How would you explain this result?

_____

_____

_____

_____

_____

Are these results involving astrologers consistent or inconsistent with the results you obtained for Hypothesis 1 above? Explain.

_____

_____

_____

_____

_____

_____

_____

_____

_____

EXERCISE 10: JOB SATISFACTION

TASKS: Mapping, Univariate, Cross-tabulation
DATA FILES: GLOBAL, SURVEY

From the start, sociologists expected that most workers in modernizing societies would resent their employers and dislike their jobs. More than a century ago, Karl Marx based his theory of the coming socialist revolution on the expectation that those who worked for wages ("wage slaves") must become dissatisfied ("estranged from their work"). As modernization caused the growth of factories and large organizations, this became the accepted view among most non-Marxist sociologists too. It seemed self-evident that most jobs are so dull and unchallenging as to provide workers with no sense of pride or sense of accomplishment. Efforts by social scientists to document this view soon made job satisfaction one of the leading topics of empirical research. By the mid-1970s, hundreds of such studies had been reported. In the past several decades, there has been far less research on job satisfaction—mainly because the findings have been so consistent.

Rather than tell you what these studies showed, in this exercise you will find out for yourself (your results will be fully in accord with what others have found). Be prepared for some surprises.

OPEN FILE: GLOBAL

Perhaps the best way to begin is with international comparisons.

MAPPING: 56) WORK PRIDE

WORK PRIDE -- PERCENT WHO TAKE "A GREAT DEAL OF PRIDE" IN THEIR WORK (WVS)

The World Values Surveys asked people in 40 nations, "How much pride, if any, do you take in the work that you do?" Here we see the percentage in each nation who said they took a "great deal of pride" in their work.

RANK	CASE NAME	VALUE
1	United States	86
2	United Kingdom	84
3	Denmark	78
3	Ireland	78
5	Iceland	76
6	Canada	74
7	Sweden	72
7	Portugal	72
9	South Africa	68
10	Argentina	66

American workers are most likely to take great pride in their work—the overwhelming majority (86 percent) say they do. The British worker is second, while Danish and Irish workers are tied for third. In Mexico half of the workers say they take great pride in their work, but only a third do so in Japan and only small minorities in South Korea, China, Russia—only 8 percent of Latvian workers gave this answer.

As noted above, modernization was seen as the key factor in the alienation of workers causing them to lose their occupational pride and to become unhappy with work. It seemed nearly self-evident that people working in a shoe factory, who performed only one small task in the process of making shoes, could not take pride in their work in the same way as preindustrial shoemakers who made each pair of shoes from start to finish.

Hypothesis: *Worker pride will be lower, the more economically developed the nation.*

COMPARING MAPS:
    Variable 1: 56) WORK PRIDE
    Variable 2: 50) ECON DEVEL

WORK PRIDE -- PERCENT WHO TAKE "A GREAT DEAL OF PRIDE" IN THEIR WORK (WVS)

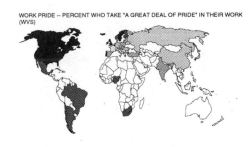

r = −0.118

ECON DEVEL -- LEVEL OF ECONOMIC DEVELOPMENT (HDR)

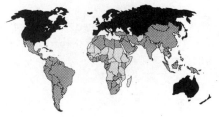

But it isn't so. There is no significant correlation. Workers in the most developed nations are not less (or more) likely to take pride in their work.

One of the key contrasts made by social scientists about work was between urban and rural workers. It was thought somehow that no one loved their work so much as peasants tending their fields and flocks.

Hypothesis: *Worker pride will be higher, the higher the percentage of the labor force employed in agriculture.*

COMPARING MAPS:
> **Variable 1:** 56) WORK PRIDE
> **Variable 2:** 66) % IN AGR.

WORK PRIDE -- PERCENT WHO TAKE "A GREAT DEAL OF PRIDE" IN THEIR WORK (WVS)

r = −0.183

% IN AGR. -- Percent of labor force employed in agriculture (TWF 1994)

No! It's lower.

Hypothesis: *Worker pride will be lower, the higher the percentage of the labor force living in urban areas.*

COMPARING MAPS:
> **Variable 1:** 56) WORK PRIDE
> **Variable 2:** 20) %URBAN

WORK PRIDE -- PERCENT WHO TAKE "A GREAT DEAL OF PRIDE" IN THEIR WORK (WVS)

r = 0.133

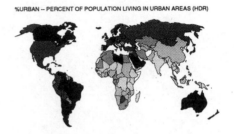

%URBAN -- PERCENT OF POPULATION LIVING IN URBAN AREAS (HDR)

Wrong again. The traditional expectations about work don't seem to stand up.

Whatever else affected work, however, it long was generally expected that unions would diminish dissatisfaction by giving employees fairer wages and greater control over their jobs.

Hypothesis: *Worker pride will be higher to the extent that workers are unionized.*

COMPARING MAPS:
> **Variable 1:** 56) WORK PRIDE
> **Variable 2:** 62) UNIONIZED?

WORK PRIDE -- PERCENT WHO TAKE "A GREAT DEAL OF PRIDE" IN THEIR WORK (WVS)

r = –0.105

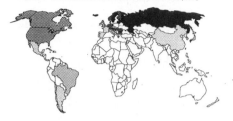

UNIONIZED? -- PERCENT WHO BELONG TO A LABOR UNION (WVS)

But this isn't so either. Nations with more of their labor force belonging to unions do not have higher levels of worker pride.

Recall which nations had the lowest levels of worker pride. In addition to the fact that many of them recently were part of or controlled by the former Soviet Union, what they tend to have in common is an economy highly regulated by the government (as in the case of China) or closely controlled by a few powerful firms, as in the case of South Korea and Japan. Does this influence worker pride? In recent years, some social scientists have argued that it does. Their reasoning is that to the extent that an economy is based on a free market within which firms must compete not only for customers, but also for talented and loyal employees, people will respond positively.

Each nation was scored from 1 to 6 in terms of the degree to which it has a regulated economy as opposed to a free market (6 indicates a very regulated economy).

Hypothesis: *Worker pride will be lower to the extent that the economy is regulated.*

COMPARING MAPS:
      Variable 1: 56) WORK PRIDE
      Variable 2: 63) ECON REG.

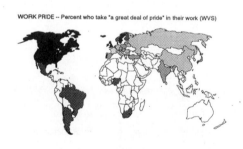

WORK PRIDE -- Percent who take "a great deal of pride" in their work (WVS)

$r = -0.548**$

ECON REG. -- DEGREE TO WHICH THE ECONOMY IS A FREE MARKET OR STATE REGULATED; 1 = LEAST REGULATED (FITW)

Exercise 10: Job Satisfaction

Yes! There is a strong, negative correlation between regulation and pride. The more regulated, the fewer workers who take pride in their work.

Now, let's take a more micro view of job satisfaction.

OPEN FILE: SURVEY

UNIVARIATE: 54) JOB SATISF

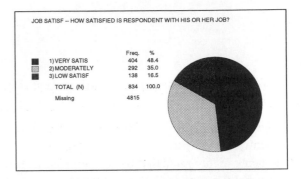

Only in the 1998 survey Americans were asked how satisfied or dissatisfied they were with the work they do. Nearly half said they were very satisfied. Added together, those who are very or moderately satisfied equal the percentage of Americans who take great pride in their work, as reported in the GLOBAL data file above.

UNIVARIATE: 30) WORK IF$$

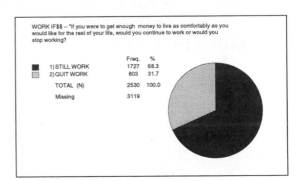

Here is a very clever way to assess how attached people are to their jobs: "If you were to get enough money to live as comfortably as you would like for the rest of your life, would you continue to work or would you stop working?" Contrary to all the commercials showing lottery winners rushing off to lead sybaritic lives, most Americans reject that option. Only a third said they would quit work if they became rich.

Hypothesis: *The more satisfied with their jobs, the more likely people are to say they would still work even if they got rich.*

Doing Sociology

CROSS-TABULATION:
Row Variable: 30) WORK IF$$
Column Variable: 54) JOB SATISF
Column%

WORK IF$$ by   JOB SATISF
Cramer's V: 0.122 *

		JOB SATISF				
		VERY SATIS	MODERATELY	LOW SATISF	Missing	TOTAL
WORK IF$$	STILL WORK	187	119	44	1377	350
		71.6%	67.2%	55.0%		67.6%
	QUIT WORK	74	58	36	635	168
		28.4%	32.8%	45.0%		32.4%
	Missing	143	115	58	2803	3119
	TOTAL	261	177	80	4815	518
		100.0%	100.0%	100.0%		

While the hypothesis is confirmed, its underlying assumptions are questioned by these results. Even most people (55.0 percent) who said they had low job satisfaction said they would go on working even if they became rich. Perhaps they would switch jobs, but they surely are not really so dissatisfied with work as such.

If, for years, it was widely assumed that the modern wage worker was unhappy, today it is equally taken for granted that women tend to resent their work situations.

Hypothesis: *Men are more likely than women to be satisfied with their jobs and to say they would still work even if they got rich.*

CROSS-TABULATION:
Row Variable: 54) JOB SATISF
Column Variable: 3) SEX
Column%

JOB SATISF   by   SEX
Cramer's V: 0.088 *

		SEX		
		MALE	FEMALE	TOTAL
JOB SATISF	VERY SATIS	173	231	404
		45.8%	50.7%	48.4%
	MODERATELY	129	163	292
		34.1%	35.7%	35.0%
	LOW SATISF	76	62	138
		20.1%	13.6%	16.5%
	Missing	2083	2732	4815
	TOTAL	378	456	834
		100.0%	100.0%	

CROSS-TABULATION:
Row Variable: 30) WORK IF$$
Column Variable: 3) SEX
Column%

WORK IF$$ by   SEX
Cramer's V: 0.037

		SEX		
		MALE	FEMALE	TOTAL
WORK IF$$	STILL WORK	858	869	1727
	QUIT WORK	367	436	803
	Missing	1236	1883	3119
	TOTAL	1225	1305	2530

Another obvious hypothesis turns out to be obviously wrong!

Your turn.

WORKSHEET

NAME: _____

COURSE: _____

DATE: _____

EXERCISE

10

REVIEW QUESTIONS

Based on the first part of this exercise, answer True or False to the following items:

Compared with Americans, Japanese workers take less pride in their work.	T F
Early sociologists believed that modernization would result in a more satisfied work force.	T F
Worker satisfaction is currently one of the most active areas of sociological research.	T F
Most Americans would not continue to work if they didn't need the money.	T F
Women are less satisfied with their jobs than are men.	T F

> **OPEN FILE:** SURVEY

1. **Hypothesis:** *The higher their income, the more satisfied people will be with their jobs.*

CROSS-TABULATION:
    ROW VARIABLE: 54) JOB SATISF
  COLUMN VARIABLE: 10) FAMILY $
        Column %

Copy the first row of the percentaged table:

10) FAMILY $

	UNDER $15K	$15–$29K	$30–$49K	$50–$90K	OVER $90K
VERY SATIS	_____%	_____%	_____%	_____%	_____%

Which group is most apt to be very satisfied?   _____

What is the value of V for this table?   V = _____

Is V statistically significant?   Yes   No

Is the hypothesis supported or rejected?   Supported   Rejected

2. **Hypothesis:** *The higher their income, the less likely people are to say they would stop working if they no longer needed the money.*

CROSS-TABULATION:
    ROW VARIABLE: 30) WORK IF$$
    COLUMN VARIABLE: 10) FAMILY $
        Column %

Copy the first row of the percentaged table:

10) FAMILY $

	UNDER $15K	$15–$29K	$30–$49K	$50–$90K	OVER $90K
STILL WORK	_____%	_____%	_____%	_____%	_____%

Which group is most apt to say they would still work?   _____

What is the value of V for this table?   V = _____

Is V statistically significant?   Yes   No

Is the hypothesis supported or rejected?   Supported   Rejected

On the basis of these results, discuss this conclusion: Income has surprisingly little effect on job satisfaction.

_____

_____

_____

_____

_____

3. **Hypothesis:** *Union members will be more satisfied with their jobs than non-union workers.*

CROSS-TABULATION:
    ROW VARIABLE: 54) JOB SATISF
    COLUMN VARIABLE: 18) UNION MEMB
        Column %

Copy the first row of the percentaged table:

18) UNION MEMB

	UNION MEMB	NON-UNION
VERY SATIS	_____%	_____%

Which group is most apt to be very satisfied?   _____

What is the value of V for this table?   V = _____

Is V statistically significant?   Yes   No

Is the hypothesis supported or rejected?   Supported   Rejected

4. **Hypothesis:** *Union members will be less apt to quit their jobs if they no longer needed the money.*

CROSS-TABULATION:
    ROW VARIABLE: 30) WORK IF$$
  COLUMN VARIABLE: 18) UNION MEMB
       Column %

Copy the first row of the percentaged table:

18) UNION MEMB

	UNION MEMB	NON-UNION
STILL WORK	_____%	_____%

Which group is most apt to say they would still work?   _____

What is the value of V for this table?   V = _____

Is V statistically significant?   Yes   No

Is the hypothesis supported or rejected?   Supported   Rejected

5. **Hypothesis:** *The higher their level of education, the more satisfied people will be with their jobs.*

CROSS-TABULATION:
      ROW VARIABLE: 54) JOB SATISF
  COLUMN VARIABLE: 12) EDUCATION
        Column %

Copy the first row of the percentaged table:

12) EDUCATION

	NOT HS GRAD	HS GRAD	COLLEGE	GRAD SCHOOL
VERY SATIS	_____%	_____%	_____%	_____%

Which group is the most apt to be very satisfied?   _____

Which group is the least apt to be very satisfied?   _____

What is the value of V for this table?   V = _____

Is V statistically significant?   Yes   No

Is the hypothesis supported or rejected?   Supported   Rejected

6. **Hypothesis:** *The higher their level of education, the less likely people are to say they would stop working if they no longer needed the money.*

CROSS-TABULATION:
      ROW VARIABLE: 30) WORK IF$$
  COLUMN VARIABLE: 12) EDUCATION
        Column %

Copy the first row of the percentaged table:

12) EDUCATION

	NOT HS GRAD	HS GRAD	COLLEGE	GRAD SCHOOL
STILL WORK	_____%	_____%	_____%	_____%

Which group is most apt to say they would still work?   _____

Which group is least apt to say they would still work?   _____

What is the value of V for this table?   V = _____

Is V statistically significant?   Yes   No

Is the hypothesis supported or rejected?   Supported   Rejected

On the basis of these results, discuss this conclusion: Education has surprisingly little effect on job satisfaction.

_____

_____

_____

_____

_____

7.   **Hypothesis:** *The younger they are, the more satisfied people will be with their jobs.*

CROSS-TABULATION:
     ROW VARIABLE: 54) JOB SATIS
     COLUMN VARIABLE: 6) AGE
              Column %

Copy the first row of the percentaged table:

6) AGE	18–29	30–39	40–49	50–65	OVER 65
VERY SATIS	_____%	_____%	_____%	_____%	_____%

Which group is most apt to be very satisfied?   _____

Which group is least apt to be very satisfied?   _____

What is the value of V for this table?   V = _____

Is V statistically significant?   Yes   No

Is the hypothesis supported or rejected?   Supported   Rejected

How would you explain this age pattern?

_____

_____

_____

_____

_____

8. **Hypothesis:** *The younger they are, the less likely people are to say they would stop working if they no longer needed the money.*

CROSS-TABULATION:
    ROW VARIABLE: 30) WORK IF$$
  COLUMN VARIABLE: 6) AGE
         Column %

Copy the first row of the percentaged table:

6) AGE	18–29	30–39	40–49	50–65	OVER 65
STILL WORK	_____%	_____%	_____%	_____%	_____%

What is the value of V for this table?   V = _____

Is V statistically significant?   Yes   No

Is the hypothesis supported or rejected?   Supported   Rejected

How would you explain this age pattern?

_____

_____

_____

_____

_____

9. **Hypothesis:** *African American workers will be less satisfied with their jobs than will whites.*

CROSS-TABULATION:
     ROW VARIABLE: 54) JOB SATISF
COLUMN VARIABLE: 5) WH/AF-AMER
        Column %

Copy the first row of the percentaged table:

5) WH/AF-AMER

	WHITE	AFRICAN-AM
VERY SATIS	_____%	_____%

What is the value of V for this table?   V = _____

Is V statistically significant?   Yes   No

Is the hypothesis supported or rejected?   Supported   Rejected

10. **Hypothesis:** *African American workers will be more apt to quit their jobs if they no longer needed the money.*

CROSS-TABULATION:
     ROW VARIABLE: 30) WORK IF$$
COLUMN VARIABLE: 5) WH/AF-AMER
        Column %

Copy the first row of the percentaged table:

5) WH/AF-AMER

	WHITE	AFRICAN-AM
STILL WORK	_____%	_____%

What is the value of V for this table?   V = _____

Is V statistically significant?   Yes   No

Is the hypothesis supported or rejected?   Supported   Rejected

How would you interpret these results as to job satisfaction in America?

_____

_____

_____

_____

_____

_____

EXERCISE 11:
A CENTURY OF TRENDS

TASKS: Historical Trends
DATA FILES: HISTORY

The twentieth century encompassed extraordinary changes. When it began there was no air travel, no radio or television, no movies, tens of thousands of people died every year of communicable diseases that no one gets anymore, and most people did not attend high school.

In this exercise you will plot many of these changes with time series data. This refers to plotting data on the same variable over time (hence, a time series) and sometimes involves comparisons of two or more trend lines.

OPEN FILE: HISTORY

HISTORICAL TRENDS: 2) POPULATION

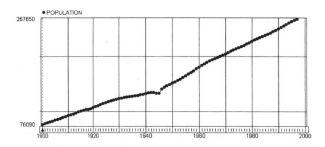

Probably the single most important change over the twentieth century is the growth of the population. In 1900, there were only about 76 million Americans. Now there are more than 276 million. The growth of the population is a smooth upward curve, except for one spot. Notice that in the early 1940s growth ceased and the population actually declined slightly. Why?

Place the mouse arrow on 1939 along the lower frame of the graphic and click. This box will appear (as shown on the next page).

Note: You also can explore the Event Box along the bottom of the screen by clicking on any event to have it marked on the screen.

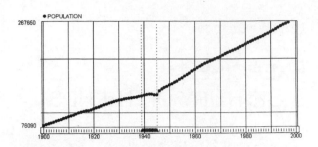

These two lines bracket the period of World War II. It began in Europe in 1939, and America entered at the end of 1941 following the Japanese bombing of Pearl Harbor. The decline in population was not caused by members of the armed forces being killed in combat. Two other factors were responsible. First, with most of the young men in service, the birth rate fell rapidly and thus deaths due to natural causes were not so fully offset by births. Second, official population totals refer only to the resident population—people living in the United States at the time. As the war proceeded, millions of Americans went overseas on military duty. Their absence shows up in this brief population decline.

HISTORICAL TRENDS: 4) FERTILITY

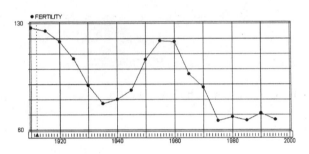

Here is the primary cause of America's immense population increase: fertility. Notice how the fertility rate declined throughout the early decades of the twentieth century. Then, in 1946 something dramatic happened. The World War II veterans came home. It's easy to see why the postwar era was called the baby boom!

Place the mouse arrow on 1950 and click. The event file tells you that this is when the birth control pill was invented. Notice that the fertility rate did not drop as a result. This is due to two things. First of all, when some new drug is discovered, it usually is a number of years before it becomes generally available, and that was true of the birth control pill. But, more important in this instance, people did not need the pill in order to reduce their fertility. Fertility had dropped to a very low level in the 1930s, long before there was a pill. The high fertility of the baby boom was not accidental. People wanted larger families and that's why they had them. We will pursue this in Exercise 13.

Doing Sociology

HISTORICAL TRENDS: 9) %<5

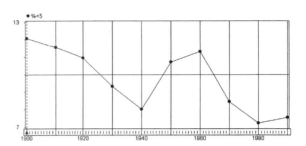

This is another way to see the baby boom—the percentage of the population under the age of five. Now let's look at both trends at the same time.

HISTORICAL TRENDS:
    Variable 1: 9) %<5
    Variable 2: 4) FERTILITY

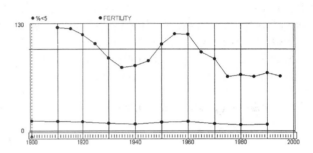

Here it looks as if there were no changes in the population under age five. That's because of the very different scales of each variable. The scale for fertility is so much larger than the one for the population under five that the large ups and downs we saw in the percentage under five are squeezed to almost nothing when both rates are examined together. This often happens, so don't be misled. However, when two variables have a sufficiently similar scale, it can be very informative to compare them on the same screen.

Fertility wasn't the only cause of population increase. A second major reason is that people began to live longer.

HISTORICAL TRENDS: 5) LIFE EXPEC

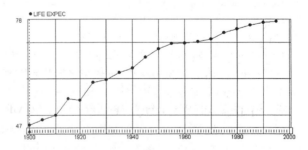

At the start of the twentieth century, the average American lived to be 47 years old. By the end of the century, life expectancy had reached 76! Notice, however, that there is a slight decline in the curve from 1915 to 1920. Why?

Exercise 11: A Century of Trends

HISTORICAL TRENDS: 28) FLU&PNEUMO

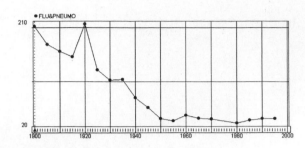

Here we have death rates from influenza (flu) and pneumonia—the latter usually being the proximate cause of deaths from flu. Notice the huge rise between 1915 and 1920. This reflects the flu epidemic of 1918 that took at least 20 million lives worldwide in just a few months. In America whole families were found dead in their homes, and more than a half million people died. Even today public health scientists aren't sure that this same flu virus would be much less deadly if it should reappear.

HISTORICAL TRENDS: 27) DIPHTHERIA

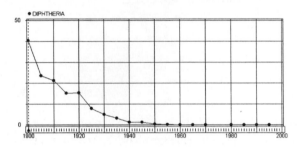

Diphtheria was once a major killer, especially of children. It was caused by a bacterial infection that blocked the air passages to the lungs. Today children are inoculated against diphtheria, and it has almost disappeared in the United States.

HISTORICAL TRENDS:
> **Variable 1:** 27) DIPHTHERIA
> **Variable 2:** 26) TB DEATHS

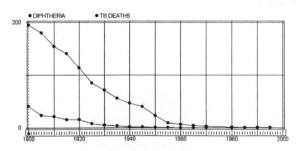

Tuberculosis was another major killer until recently. The virtual elimination of these and other, similar diseases is the primary reason life expectancy has increased so greatly. Here we are able to show both rates at once because they are sufficiently close in scale, although you will notice that the decline in diphtheria seems less dramatic since the trend is flattened somewhat on this scale.

Doing Sociology

HISTORICAL TRENDS: 11) % URBAN

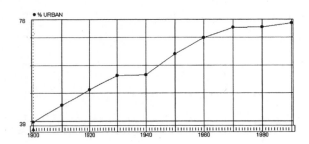

Here is another of the most significant trends of the twentieth century, although it was well underway by 1900—people moved from farms and rural villages to large urban communities. Notice, however, that the trend is flat during the 1930s. Place the arrow on 1930 and click.

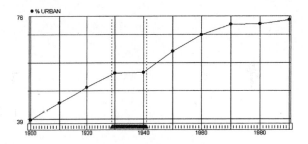

Welcome to the Great Depression. Following the stock market crash in 1929, the United States entered a decade of great poverty and unemployment (as did most of the world). As many as a third of workers were unemployed. And, while the Depression lasted, a lot of trends stopped. In this instance, people stopped moving to urban areas, being content to stay in rural areas and small towns where they at least had close social ties to help them sustain this period of privation.

Your turn.

EXERCISE 12:
DIFFUSION AND CULTURAL COMPLEXITY

TASKS: Mapping, Univariate, Cross-tabulation
DATA FILES: GLOBAL, XCULT

In the 1400s, as early explorers began to venture out of Europe—first circumnavigating Africa to reach Asia and later discovering the Western Hemisphere—they found a world of amazing technological and cultural contrasts. Some societies could produce steel while others couldn't work metal of any kind. Some societies could weave fine cloth, others could clothe themselves only in animal skins. Some societies published books and produced great works of literature, others had no written language.

Today, after more than 500 years of progress, the contrasts are still extreme. Some societies manufacture airplanes, while others don't even have an airport. Indeed, there are still many societies without a written language.

Even among the larger societies, immense contrasts remain.

OPEN FILE: GLOBAL

MAPPING: 11) TV SETS

TV SETS -- NUMBER OF TV SETS PER 1,000 POPULATION (HDR)

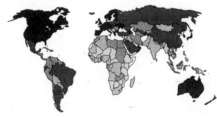

This map shows the international distribution of TV sets.

LIST RANK

RANK	CASE NAME	VALUE
1	Bahamas	896
2	United States	847
3	Qatar	808
4	Canada	715
5	Japan	707
6	United Kingdom	645
7	Finland	640
8	Australia	639
9	Brunei	638
10	Luxembourg	619

The Bahamas have the most TV sets, having nearly nine sets for every ten people. The United States is a close second. In Malawi and Chad, there are only two sets per 1,000 people.

MAPPING: 53) ELECTRIC

ELECTRIC -- PER CAPITA ANNUAL ELECTRICITY CONSUMPTION [IN KILOWATT HOURS] (TWF)

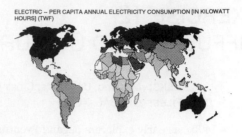

One reason some nations lack TVs is that they also have very little electricity and even that limited supply is unreliably available.

LIST RANK

RANK	CASE NAME	VALUE
1	Norway	24586
2	Iceland	17181
3	Canada	16137
4	Sweden	14862
5	Luxembourg	13443
6	Kuwait	12793
7	Finland	12373
8	United States	11636
9	Qatar	10095
10	New Zealand	9198

Norway, with an abundance of dams, leads the world in electricity production with 24,586 kilowatt-hours per person per year. Canada produces 16,137 kilowatt-hours, Chad produces 14.

MAPPING: 56) CARS/1000

CARS/1000 -- NUMBER OF AUTOMOBILES PER 1000 POPULATION (WA)

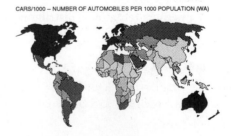

Automobiles also are very unevenly distributed around the world.

Doing Sociology

LIST RANK

RANK	CASE NAME	VALUE
1	Italy	546.4
2	Luxembourg	540.0
3	Germany	503.5
4	United States	489.1
5	Iceland	464.4
6	Austria	463.2
7	Australia	456.4
8	Switzerland	452.0
9	Brunei	452.0
10	Belgium	434.1

Italy has the most automobiles per 1,000—more than one for every two people. Then come Luxembourg, Germany, and the United States. In Cuba there are only 1.5 cars per 1,000 people. That means that in a city of 100,000 people, there would be only 150 cars. In Myanmar, a city of 100,000 would have only 70 cars.

From the earliest days of exploration, the question has been, Why are some societies so much more advanced than others? Or, put another way, How does cultural and technological development occur?

It might seem that the answer to that question would involve an explanation of innovation—how are new technologies invented? But that's not the factor social scientists would mention first. Instead, they would point out that most of any society's culture, including its technology, was not discovered or created by a member of that society. Most of it came from outside.

As the famous anthropologist Ralph Linton explained back in 1936, "The number of successful inventions within . . . any one society . . . is always small. If every human group had been left to climb upward by its own unaided efforts, progress would have been so slow that it is doubtful whether any society by now would have advanced beyond the level of the Old Stone Age."

More rapid progress was achieved because societies borrow innovations from one another. The process by which innovations are transferred from one society to another is called *diffusion*. This hypothesis follows: Societies with greater opportunity for diffusion will have more complex culture and more powerful technology.

How can we measure the opportunity for diffusion? Clearly, this ought to involve the extent of communication and contact with other societies.

It frequently has been pointed out that sea travel has played a major role in development precisely because for so long it was the most efficient means of transportation. Seafaring nations have had more contact with other societies and thus have enjoyed a considerable advantage over landlocked societies in terms of diffusion.

Exercise 12: Diffusion and Cultural Complexity

COASTLINE -- LENGTH OF COASTLINE IN KILOMETERS (TWF)

This variable gives us a rough approximation of access to the sea as a factor in diffusion—it is the number of kilometers of coastline for each of these 174 nations (1 mile equals 1.6 kilometers). Because they include a huge number of islands, two nations have seacoasts far out of proportion to all other nations. Canada's total coastline is 243,791 kilometers and Indonesia has 54,716 kilometers of seacoast. Being so off-scale, these two nations crush the results. To deal with this problem, both nations have been coded as missing data on this measure and therefore do not influence any of the following correlations.

LIST RANK

RANK	CASE NAME	VALUE
1	Russia	37653
2	Philippines	36289
3	Japan	29751
4	Australia	25760
5	Norway	21925
6	United States	19924
7	New Zealand	15134
8	China	14500
9	Greece	13676
10	United Kingdom	12429

With Canada and Indonesia omitted, Russia has the longest coastline—37,653 kilometers; the U.S. coastline is 19,924 kilometers. Notice that many nations have no coastline at all.

If coastline is a valid measure of the opportunity for diffusion, then a number of hypotheses should hold.

Hypothesis: *Length of coastline ought to be positively correlated with the prevalence of TV sets.*

Doing Sociology

COMPARING MAPS:
      Variable 1: 52) COASTLINE
      Variable 2: 11) TV SETS

COASTLINE -- LENGTH OF COASTLINE IN KILOMETERS (TWF)

r = 0.321**

TV SETS -- NUMBER OF TV SETS PER 1,000 POPULATION (HDR)

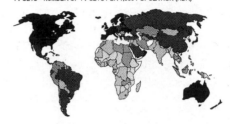

And so it is.

Hypothesis: *Length of coastline ought to be positively correlated with the prevalence of electricity.*

COMPARING MAPS:
      Variable 1: 52) COASTLINE
      Variable 2: 53) ELECTRIC

COASTLINE -- LENGTH OF COASTLINE IN KILOMETERS (TWF)

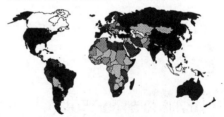

r = 0.329**

ELECTRIC -- PER CAPITA ANNUAL ELECTRICITY CONSUMPTION [IN KILOWATT HOURS] (TWF)

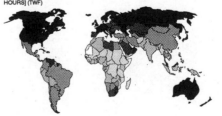

Right again.

Exercise 12: Diffusion and Cultural Complexity

Hypothesis: *Length of coastline ought to be positively correlated with the prevalence of cars.*

COMPARING MAPS:
      Variable 1: 52) COASTLINE
      Variable 2: 26) CARS/1000

COASTLINE -- LENGTH OF COASTLINE IN KILOMETERS (TWF)

r = 0.260**

CARS/1000 -- NUMBER OF AUTOMOBILES PER 1000 POPULATION (WA)

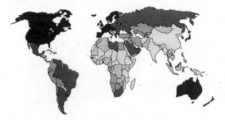

Yes.

Hypothesis: *Length of coastline ought to be positively correlated with the overall level of economic development.*

COMPARING MAPS:
      Variable 1: 52) COASTLINE
      Variable 2: 50) ECON DEVEL

COASTLINE -- LENGTH OF COASTLINE IN KILOMETERS (TWF)

r = 0.244**

ECON DEVEL -- LEVEL OF ECONOMIC DEVELOPMENT (HDR)

These findings strongly suggest that coastline is a valid measure of diffusion and that coastal nations have benefited from being easy to reach and by being able to reach other societies.

Your turn.

WORKSHEET

NAME: _____

COURSE: _____

DATE: _____

Workbook exercises and software are copyrighted. Copying is prohibited by law.

REVIEW QUESTIONS

Based on the first part of this exercise, answer True or False to the following items:

The inequalities among nations as to their economic and technological development
are relatively new—500 years ago societies were pretty much the same.   T   F

The technologically most advanced nations differ from other nations because each has
discovered and created most of its own technology.   T   F

Diffusion refers to the spread of innovations.   T   F

As of 1997, every nation now has at least one TV station.   T   F

A kilometer is just a bit longer than a mile.   T   F

OPEN FILE: XCULT

UNIVARIATE: 11) GATHER

1. The most primitive mode of human subsistence relies on gathering food that grows wild.

    What percentage of these societies have much dependence on gathering?   _____%

    UNIVARIATE: 12) WHEELS

2. Wheels provide a far more efficient form of transportation, compared with using pack animals or people carrying everything on their backs.

    What percentage of these societies have the wheel?   _____%

    UNIVARIATE: 13) WORK METAL

3. One of the great leaps forward in human technology was learning to make metal tools instead of relying on stone and bone.

    What percentage of these societies know how to work metal?   _____%

Exercise 12: Diffusion and Cultural Complexity   177

UNIVARIATE: 2) WRITING

4. Writing enables human societies to "remember" what they know and to easily transmit it.

What percentage of these societies have writing?   _____%

UNIVARIATE: 14) C.COMPLEX.

5. Social scientists often combine many variables to create a more accurate measure, often called an index or a scale. This index combines some of the above and other aspects of culture to measure each society's level of cultural complexity.

What percentage of these societies score in the lower level?   _____%

In this data file there is one variable that is an excellent measure of the opportunity for diffusion. Please identify this variable.

6. Name of variable: _____

Its description:

_____

_____

7. Explain why this is a measure of the opportunity for diffusion to occur.

_____

_____

_____

_____

_____

8. Now, use this variable to test this **hypothesis:** *The greater the opportunity for diffusion, the more advanced the culture and technology.*

CROSS-TABULATION:
ROW VARIABLE: 11) GATHER
COLUMN VARIABLE: _____
    Column %

Doing Sociology

What is the value of V for this table?   V = _____

Is V statistically significant?   Yes   No

Is the hypothesis supported or rejected?   Supported   Rejected

9. **CROSS-TABULATION:**
    ROW VARIABLE: 12) WHEELS
COLUMN VARIABLE: _____
        Column %

What is the value of V for this table?   V = _____

Is V statistically significant?   Yes   No

Is the hypothesis supported or rejected?   Supported   Rejected

10. **CROSS-TABULATION:**
    ROW VARIABLE: 13) WORK METAL
COLUMN VARIABLE: _____
        Column %

What is the value of V for this table?   V = _____

Is V statistically significant?   Yes   No

Is the hypothesis supported or rejected?   Supported   Rejected

11. **CROSS-TABULATION:**
    ROW VARIABLE: 2) WRITING
COLUMN VARIABLE: _____
        Column %

What is the value of V for this table?   V = _____

Is V statistically significant?   Yes   No

Is the hypothesis supported or rejected?   Supported   Rejected

12. **CROSS-TABULATION:**
   ROW VARIABLE: 14) C.COMPLEX.
   COLUMN VARIABLE: _____
   Column %

What is the value of V for this table?   V = _____

Is V statistically significant?   Yes   No

Is the hypothesis supported or rejected?   Supported   Rejected

EXERCISE 13:
FERTILITY

TASKS: Mapping
DATA FILES: GLOBAL

For most of the latter half of the twentieth century, all discussions of fertility were focused on rapid population *growth*. The term *population explosion* dominated both the scholarly and the popular discussions of fertility. Then came a substantial shift as in most societies fertility rates fell rapidly. While there still is concern about population growth in some parts of the world, the latest concern is about population *decline*.

OPEN FILE: GLOBAL

MAPPING: 13) POP GROW

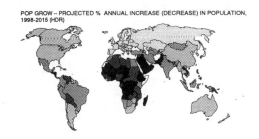

POP GROW -- PROJECTED % ANNUAL INCREASE (DECREASE) IN POPULATION, 1998-2015 (HDR)

This map shows the latest projections of annual rates of population growth or decline for 164 nations for the period 1998–2015 as prepared by demographers at the United Nations. The darkest areas, having the most rapid rates of growth, are clustered in Africa, especially south of the Sahara. In contrast, Europe is shown in the lightest shade.

CLICK ON: Legend

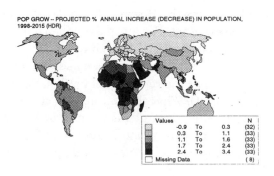

POP GROW -- PROJECTED % ANNUAL INCREASE (DECREASE) IN POPULATION, 1998-2015 (HDR)

Values			N
-0.9	To	0.3	(32)
0.3	To	1.1	(33)
1.1	To	1.6	(33)
1.7	To	2.4	(33)
2.4	To	3.4	(33)
Missing Data			(8)

Here we see that the nations with the highest rates of population growth are in the range of 2.4 to 3.4 percent. Rates this high cause populations to double in only a few years. However, most of those shown in the lightest shade have declining populations (as indicated by the minus sign)—the populations of Latvia and Estonia are shrinking by nearly 1 percent a year. That doesn't sound like much. But if a nation has a population of 10 million and its population is declining by 0.9 percent per year, in 20 years it will have only 8.3 million people and in 40 years there will be only 6.9 million.

MAPPING: 15) FERTILITY

FERTILITY – NUMBER OF BIRTHS TO THE AVERAGE WOMAN DURING HER LIFETIME

This map looks very much like the one above. The major factor in population growth or decline is fertility, measured here as the number of births to the average woman during her lifetime.

LIST RANK

RANK	CASE NAME	VALUE
1	Yemen	7.6
2	Uganda	7.1
3	Niger	6.8
3	Angola	6.8
3	Malawi	6.8
6	Mali	6.6
6	Burkina Faso	6.6
8	Congo, Dem. Republic	6.4
9	Ethiopia	6.3
9	Burundi	6.3

Yemen has the highest rate of growth (3.4 percent per year) because it has the highest fertility rate: 7.6. Next come a long list of Sub-Saharan African nations, all with fertility rates that result in rapid population growth. However, beginning with Georgia (1.9), nations have fertility rates that are below replacement level. For a population to be balanced, to neither grow nor decline, the average woman must give birth to two children (plus a fraction to offset infant and childhood mortality): one child to replace the father and one to replace the mother. Many nations, especially in Europe, have fertility rates *far below* the replacement level. In Spain the average woman is bearing only slightly more than one child (1.1). What that means is that the populations in many European nations have started to shrink rapidly. Even if this is offset by immigration, later in this century there will be few ethnic Spaniards in Spain, or ethnic Italians in Italy, for example. Moreover, if population decline is not offset by immigration, the population will very rapidly become old.

FERTILITY -- NUMBER OF BIRTHS TO THE AVERAGE WOMAN DURING HER LIFETIME

r = −0.770**

OVER 65 -- PERCENT OF POPULATION OVER 65 (HDR)

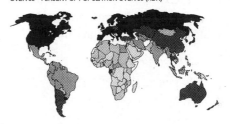

As a population becomes old, increasingly smaller cohorts of young people will struggle to support much larger cohorts of elderly. Moreover, as populations age, births must decline too since fertility is limited biologically to increasingly smaller cohorts of younger people.

Now let's explore how and why some places have such low fertility, while in other places fertility remains high.

MAPPING: 16) CONTRACEP

CONTRACEP -- PERCENT OF MARRIED WOMEN (15-49) USING A BIRTH CONTROL METHOD OR DEVICE (HDR)

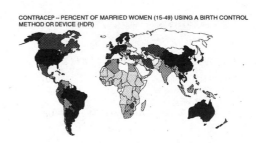

Fertility will always be high unless something is done to prevent it. The most common way to limit family size is by one or another form of contraception. Here we see variations around the world in the percentage of married women (or their husbands) in their childbearing years who are using contraception.

LIST RANK

RANK	CASE NAME	VALUE
1	Uruguay	84
2	China	83
3	United Kingdom	82
3	Cuba	82
5	Finland	80
5	Netherlands	80
7	South Korea	79
7	Belgium	79
9	Sweden	78
9	Italy	78

The percentage is highest in Uruguay (84 percent) and China is next highest. Three nations are tied for third: United Kingdom, Cuba, and Finland. The United States is twenty-second (74 percent) and in Mexico 69 percent use contraceptives. In some other nations, very few use contraception: 4 percent in Ethiopia and 1 percent in Guinea-Bissau.

MAPPING: 22) ABORTION

ABORTION – ABORTIONS PER 1,000 LIVE BIRTHS (NBWR)

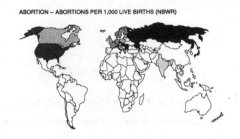

Another way to limit family size is abortion.

LIST RANK

RANK	CASE NAME	VALUE
1	Russia	2300
2	Bulgaria	1072
3	Romania	990
4	Cuba	708
5	Hungary	656
6	Czech Republic	528
7	Slovak Republic	502
8	Singapore	471
9	United States	428
10	Denmark	400

In Russia, abortion is a primary means of birth control as there are 2,300 abortions for every 1,000 births.

Doing Sociology

Variable 1: 15) FERTILITY
Variable 2: 16) CONTRACEP

FERTILITY – NUMBER OF BIRTHS TO THE AVERAGE WOMAN DURING HER LIFETIME

r = −0.881**

CONTRACEP -- PERCENT OF MARRIED WOMEN (15-49) USING A BIRTH CONTROL METHOD OR DEVICE (HDR)

This very high correlation demonstrates the obvious: that fertility rates are mainly determined by choice, by people choosing to use or not to use contraceptives. Why do people in some nations choose not to use them?

Your turn.

EXERCISE 14: REGRESSION

TASKS: Mapping, Regression
DATA FILES: GLOBAL, STATES, XCULT

Throughout this book you have tested hypotheses by seeing if one variable was correlated with another. In the previous exercise you examined the correlations between fertility and a series of other variables including infant mortality (r = 0.829) and education (r = −0.826). But suppose you wanted to examine the correlations of both variables with fertility at the same time. How much impact do they have on fertility together?

You can't calculate the answer simply by adding the two correlations together. If you did (and ignored the fact that one correlation is negative and one positive), the total would greatly exceed 1.0, which is as high as the correlation coefficient goes. The reason each can have such a high correlation with fertility is because a substantial portion of their effect is shared. That is, infant mortality rates are highly correlated with education and both the correlated portions of each as well as their independent portions influence fertility. That sounds complicated, but you soon will see that it isn't.

OPEN FILE: GLOBAL

COMPARING MAPS:
 Variable 1: 7) INF MORTAL
 Variable 2: 65) EDUCATION

INF MORTAL -- INFANT (1ST YEAR) DEATHS PER 1,000 LIVE BIRTHS (HDR)

r = −0.773**

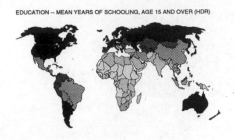

EDUCATION -- MEAN YEARS OF SCHOOLING, AGE 15 AND OVER (HDR)

The combined maps show the very high correlation between infant mortality and education. To see the independent effect of each of these variables on fertility, we use a technique called **regression**.

REGRESSION:
    Dependent Variable: 15) FERTILITY
    Independent Variable: 7) INF MORTAL
    Independent Variable: 65) EDUCATION

Multiple R-Squared = 0.765**

INF MORTAL   BETA = 0.530**   (r = 0.837)   FERTILITY

EDUCATION   BETA = -0.398**   (r = -0.807)

Each independent variable is connected to the dependent variable by a horizontal line. Below each line is the correlation between that variable and the dependent variable. Above the line is something called the BETA. BETA refers to the standardized beta, which estimates **the independent or net effect of this variable on the dependent variable**. Recall that these two independent variables are correlated with one another as well as with the dependent variable. What regression does is to sort out the independent or net contribution of each variable and express it as a value of BETA. In this instance the net effect of infant mortality on fertility is 0.530** and the net effect of education is –0.398**. Each variable has a significant net effect on fertility—we know because the two asterisks following each BETA tell us that it is significant at the .01 level.

At the upper right corner of the screen you can read: Multiple R-Squared = 0.765**. This often is written R^2 and measures **the joint or combined effects of the independent variables**. That means that together, infant mortality and education account for 76.5 percent of the variation in fertility rates. Put another way, if all nations had precisely the same infant mortality rates and precisely the same levels of education, then there would be 76.5 percent less variation in their fertility rates than there is. Notice too that Multiple R-Squared is not simply the sum of the BETAs. It is a separate calculation. And here too the question of statistical significance must be answered, and in this case the answer is a loud "yes," as indicated by the two asterisks.

REGRESSION:
    Dependent Variable: 15) FERTILITY
    Independent Variable: 26) CARS/1000
    Independent Variable: 11) TV SETS
    Independent Variable: 17) CALORIES

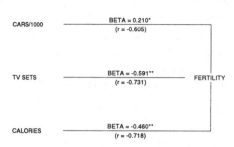

Multiple R-Squared = 0.635**

CARS/1000 — BETA = 0.210* (r = -0.605)

TV SETS — BETA = -0.591** (r = -0.731) — FERTILITY

CALORIES — BETA = -0.460** (r = -0.718)

Many independent variables can be included in the same regression, limited only by the total number of cases on which the analysis is based. As the number increases, however, the results can become difficult to interpret, so you will not be expected to use more than three, as shown above.

To see the independent or net effect of each of these aspects of modernization on fertility, examine the BETAs. Each is sizable and statistically significant, meaning each variable makes an independent contribution to accounting for fertility. The Multiple R-Squared reports the total effect of all three independent variables—together they account for 63.5 percent of variation in fertility.

REGRESSION:
    Dependent Variable: 15) FERTILITY
    Independent Variable: 66) % IN AGR.
    Independent Variable: 20) %URBAN

Multiple R-Squared = 0.592**

% IN AGR. — BETA = 0.805** (r = 0.769)

FERTILITY

%URBAN — BETA = 0.044 (r = -0.614)

Here we see something new. When the effect of agricultural employment is excluded, the percent urban has no net effect. That is, % IN AGR. has a large and significant BETA, but %URBAN does not, despite the fact that its correlation with fertility is very large.

OPEN FILE: STATES

REGRESSION:
    Dependent Variable: 19) ALCOHOL
    Independent Variable: 30) %SINGL MEN
    Independent Variable: 31) %SINGL.FEM

Multiple R-Squared = 0.159*

%SINGL MEN — BETA = 1.109** (r = 0.222)

ALCOHOL

%SINGL.FEM — BETA = -0.948* (r = 0.092)

There are several important things to observe here. In the first two examples, the BETAs are smaller than the correlations. But BETAs also **can be much larger**, as these are. What this shows is that these two independent variables are very strongly correlated with alcohol consumption, but in the opposite direction. Single males increase consumption, single females decrease it. But this does not show up in the correlations because the proportion of single males and of single females is very highly correlated—they tend to be in the same places. So, they tend to cancel one another out. Regression untangles these contrary effects, and let us see what's really going on. The second thing to observe is that, unlike correlation coefficients, **BETAs can exceed 1.0**.

OPEN FILE: XCULT

REGRESSION:
    Dependent Variable: 4) STRATIFIED
    Independent Variable: 8) FIXITY
    Independent Variable: 14) C.COMPLEX.

Multiple R-Squared = 0.437**

FIXITY — BETA = 0.234** (r = 0.428)

C.COMPLEX. — BETA = 0.540** (r = 0.624)

STRATIFIED

In Exercise 6 you discovered that both fixity and cultural complexity were significantly correlated with the degree of stratification in premodern societies. Here we see that each has a strong, independent (or net) effect and together they account for nearly half (43.7 percent) of the variation in stratification.

Your turn.

Doing Sociology

WORKSHEET

Workbook exercises and software are copyrighted. Copying is prohibited by law.

NAME:

COURSE:

DATE:

EXERCISE
14

REVIEW QUESTIONS

Based on the first part of this exercise, answer True or False to the following items:

Multiple R-Squared is the sum of the BETAs.	T F
BETA estimates the joint effect of the independent variables.	T F
BETAs can exceed 1.0.	T F
Regression analysis is used to discover the net effect of each independent variable.	T F
Regression analysis is used to discover the joint effect of a set of independent variables.	T F

OPEN FILE: STATES

1. **Hypothesis:** *Playboy circulation will be (select one)* ❑ *higher* ❑ *lower where there is a higher proportion of single men and (select one)* ❑ *higher* ❑ *lower where there is a higher proportion of single women.*

REGRESSION:
   DEPENDENT VARIABLE: 46) PLAYBOY
   INDEPENDENT VARIABLE: 30) %SINGL MEN
   INDEPENDENT VARIABLE: 31) %SINGL.FEM

What is the combined effect of these two independent variables?	_____
What is the independent effect of %SINGL MEN?	_____
Is it negative or positive?	Negative Positive
Is it significant?	Yes No
What is the independent effect of %SINGL.FEM?	_____
Is it negative or positive?	Negative Positive
Is it significant?	Yes No

Is the hypothesis supported or rejected?   Supported   Rejected

How do these findings compare with those involving alcohol consumption?   Similar   Different

Is this the result you would have expected? Explain.

_____

_____

_____

_____

_____

2. **Hypothesis:** *Abortion rates will be (select one)* ❏ *higher* ❏ *lower where more people are church members and (select one)* ❏ *higher* ❏ *lower where more people live in metropolitan areas.*

REGRESSION:
  DEPENDENT VARIABLE: 21) ABORTIONS
  INDEPENDENT VARIABLE: 14) CH.MEMBERS
  INDEPENDENT VARIABLE: 4) % METROPOL

What is the combined effect of these two independent variables?   _____

What is the independent effect of CH.MEMBERS?   _____

Is it negative or positive?   Negative   Positive

Is it significant?   Yes   No

What is the independent effect of % METROPOL?   _____

Is it negative or positive?   Negative   Positive

Is it significant?   Yes   No

Is the hypothesis supported or rejected?   Supported   Rejected

Is this the result you would have expected? If not, can you suggest why?

_____

_____

_____

_____

_____

3.   **Hypothesis:** _Ownership of pickup trucks will be (select one) ❑ higher ❑ lower where more people hunt and (select one) ❑ higher ❑ lower where more people live in metropolitan areas._

REGRESSION:
   DEPENDENT VARIABLE: 43) PICKUPS
   INDEPENDENT VARIABLE: 27) HUNTERS
   INDEPENDENT VARIABLE: 4) % METROPOL

What is the combined effect of these two independent variables?   _____

What is the independent effect of HUNTERS?   _____

Is it negative or positive?   Negative   Positive

Is it significant?   Yes   No

What is the independent effect of % METROPOL?   _____

Is it negative or positive?   Negative   Positive

Is it significant?   Yes   No

Is the hypothesis supported or rejected?   Supported   Rejected

Is this the result you would have expected? If not, can you suggest why?

_____

_____

_____

_____

_____

OPEN FILE: GLOBAL

4. **Hypothesis:** *Average life expectancy will be (select one)* ❑ *higher* ❑ *lower where the average person eats more calories and (select one)* ❑ *higher* ❑ *lower where people eat more meat.*

REGRESSION:
  DEPENDENT VARIABLE: 2) LIFE EXPEC
  INDEPENDENT VARIABLE: 17) CALORIES
  INDEPENDENT VARIABLE: 25) MEAT CONS.

What is the combined effect of these two independent variables?   _____

What is the independent effect of CALORIES?   _____

Is it negative or positive?   Negative   Positive

Is it significant?   Yes   No

What is the independent effect of MEAT CONS.?   _____

Is it negative or positive?   Negative   Positive

Is it significant?   Yes   No

Is the hypothesis supported or rejected?   Supported   Rejected

Is this the result you predicted? If not, can you suggest why?

_____

_____

_____

_____

_____

Doing Sociology

5. **Hypothesis:** *Average life expectancy will be (select one)* ❑ *higher* ❑ *lower where the average person eats more calories and (select one)* ❑ *higher* ❑ *lower where more people smoke.*

REGRESSION:
    DEPENDENT VARIABLE: 2) LIFE EXPEC
    INDEPENDENT VARIABLE: 17) CALORIES
    INDEPENDENT VARIABLE: 10) CIGARETTES

    What is the combined effect of these two independent variables?   _____

    What is the independent effect of CALORIES?   _____

    Is it negative or positive?   Negative   Positive

    Is it significant?   Yes   No

    What is the independent effect of CIGARETTES?   _____

    Is it negative or positive?   Negative   Positive

    Is it significant?   Yes   No

    Is the hypothesis supported or rejected?   Supported   Rejected

  Is this the result you predicted? If not, can you suggest why?

_____

_____

_____

_____

_____

6. **Hypothesis:** *Average life expectancy will be (select one)* ❑ *higher* ❑ *lower where more people use drugs and (select one)* ❑ *higher* ❑ *lower where people drink more alcohol.*

REGRESSION:
    DEPENDENT VARIABLE: 2) LIFE EXPEC
    INDEPENDENT VARIABLE: 29) DRUG USE
    INDEPENDENT VARIABLE: 28) ALCOHOL

What is the combined effect of these two independent variables? _____

What is the independent effect of DRUG USE? _____

Is it negative or positive?   Negative   Positive

Is it significant?   Yes   No

What is the independent effect of ALCOHOL? _____

Is it negative or positive?   Negative   Positive

Is it significant?   Yes   No

Is the hypothesis supported or rejected?   Supported   Rejected

Is this the result you predicted? If not, can you suggest why?

_____

_____

_____

_____

_____

Doing Sociology

EXERCISE 15:
SPURIOUSNESS

TASKS: Cross-tabulation, Mapping, Regression
DATA FILES: COLLEGE, GLOBAL, STATES

The news media frequently report the results of social science research. Some of these stories are based on well-done studies based on good samples, careful analysis, and good judgment. Others never should have been published. In this exercise you are going to learn a little trick that will help you spot reports that are unlikely to be trustworthy.

There is nothing involved that you don't already understand. Suppose I told you that research found that among adults, the average tall person likes football better than the average short person. After a moment of reflection you might say, "Well sure, most tall people are men. All you're saying is that men like football better than women do." And that's it. That's all this exercise is about.

Let's start with a newspaper story:

Criminals Don't Wear Rings

Researchers have discovered that people who wear rings are much less likely to have been in trouble with the police.

Speaking before a huge press conference, Dr. Dewey Dingledubber, the well-known criminologist from the Massachusetts Institute of Sanitation, revealed that "people who wear one ring are less criminal than those who wear none." He went on to say that "those who wear two rings have even cleaner records."

"Right now I can't completely explain this," Dr. Dingledubber told his amazed listeners. "Maybe people who wear more rings have too strong a sense of fashion to go around committing silly offenses."

When informed of Dingledubber's results, Dr. Jake Judo of the Michigan College of Lake Management said he was not surprised. "Cops are impressed by flashy jewelry and they don't arrest people who impress them. This is just another example of police bias."

CROSS-TABULATION:
Row Variable: 3) PICKED UP?
Column Variable: 2) RINGS
Column %

PICKED UP?   by   RINGS
Cramer's V: 0.110 *

		RINGS				
		2 OR MORE	ONE	NEVER	Missing	TOTAL
PICKED UP?	PICKED UP	19	65	56	2	140
		11.6%	20.4%	23.1%		19.3%
	NO	145	254	186	11	585
		88.4%	79.6%	76.9%		80.7%
	Missing	1	3	0	19	23
	TOTAL	164	319	242	32	725
		100.0%	100.0%	100.0%		

These are the results that got Dr. Dingledubber into the news. People who do not wear rings are the ones most apt to have been picked up by the police. Those who wear two rings are least likely to have been picked up. And the finding is statistically significant. What else could Dr. Dingledubber have done except to announce his amazing findings? He might have stopped to think.

Is there anything *else* about people who tend to wear rings that is different from those who tend not to? Could it be something that is the *real cause* of this result? Well, what about sex?

CROSS-TABULATION:
Row Variable: 2) RINGS
Column Variable: 1) SEX
Column %

RINGS   by   SEX
Cramer's V: 0.604 **

		SEX			
		Female	Male	Missing	TOTAL
RINGS	2 OR MORE	152	12	1	164
		38.2%	3.6%		22.6%
	ONE	210	111	1	321
		52.8%	33.7%		44.2%
	NEVER	36	206	0	242
		9.0%	62.6%		33.3%
	Missing	2	1	29	32
	TOTAL	398	329	31	727
		100.0%	100.0%		

Clearly, females tend to be the ones who wear rings. We wouldn't be surprised to discover that males are more likely to have been picked up by the police. And that's what Dr. Dingledubber really discovered.

CROSS-TABULATION:
Row Variable: 3) PICKED UP?
Column Variable: 2) RINGS
Control Variable: 1) SEX
Column %

PICKED UP?   by   RINGS
Controls: SEX: Female
Cramer's V: 0.042

		RINGS				
		2 OR MORE	ONE	NEVER	Missing	TOTAL
PICKED UP?	PICKED UP	16	26	3	0	45
		10.6%	12.5%	8.3%		11.4%
	NO	135	182	33	2	350
		89.4%	87.5%	91.7%		88.6%
	Missing	1	2	0	0	3
	TOTAL	151	208	36	2	395
		100.0%	100.0%	100.0%		

This first table is limited to females. There no longer is any consistent or significant effect of ring-wearing in this group.

PICKED UP?   by   RINGS
Controls: SEX: Male
Cramer's V: 0.102

		2 OR MORE	ONE	NEVER	Missing	TOTAL
	PICKED UP	3	39	53	0	95
		25.0%	35.5%	25.7%		29.0%
	NO	9	71	153	1	233
		75.0%	64.5%	74.3%		71.0%
	Missing	0	1	0	0	1
	TOTAL	12	110	206	1	328
		100.0%	100.0%	100.0%		

This second table is limited to males. The same thing here: no ring effect (ignore the first column since only 12 men wore 2 or more rings).

The original relationship between rings and having a police record is what is called a **spurious** relationship. Such relationships do not represent cause-and-effect, but exist only because they share a cause. In this case, sex is a cause of both ring-wearing and getting in trouble with the police.

Spurious relationships disappear when the real cause is held constant and not allowed to vary. In this case, gender is held constant when we examine groups of one gender. And within each gender group, the relationship disappeared.

Trouble is, guys like Dingledubber never quit. Soon he was in the press again.

Top of the News

Ring-Wearers Prefer Literature to Science

Dr. Dewey Dingledubber, who amazed the scientific world last month with his discovery that people who wear rings seldom have criminal records, today told the world that people who wear rings prefer literature to science.

"I guess you could say that people with good taste wear rings and that doesn't include nerds. Maybe rings get in the way in things like chemistry," he added.

CROSS-TABULATION:
  Row Variable: 4) LIT OR SCI
  Column Variable: 2) RINGS
  Column %

LIT OR SCI   by   RINGS
Cramer's V: 0.179 **

		2 OR MORE	ONE	NEVER	Missing	TOTAL
LIT OR SCI	LITERATURE	108	166	99	5	373
		65.5%	51.9%	41.1%		51.4%
	SCIENCE	57	154	142	7	353
		34.5%	48.1%	58.9%		48.6%
	Missing	0	2	1	20	23
	TOTAL	165	320	241	32	726
		100.0%	100.0%	100.0%		

Well, he's right. People who wear rings are more apt to favor literature. BUT . . .

CROSS-TABULATION:
  Row Variable: 4) LIT OR SCI
  Column Variable: 2) RINGS
  Control Variable: 1) SEX
  Column %

LIT OR SCI   by   RINGS
Controls: SEX: Female
Cramer's V: 0.065

		2 OR MORE	ONE	NEVER	Missing	TOTAL
LIT OR SCI	LITERATURE	101	125	22	1	248
		66.4%	59.8%	61.1%		62.5%
	SCIENCE	51	84	14	1	149
		33.6%	40.2%	38.9%		37.5%
	Missing	0	1	0	0	1
	TOTAL	152	209	36	2	397
		100.0%	100.0%	100.0%		

This first table is limited to females. There no longer is any consistent or significant effect of ring-wearing in this group.

LIT OR SCI   by   RINGS
Controls: SEX: Male
Cramer's V: 0.049

		2 OR MORE	ONE	NEVER	Missing	TOTAL
LIT OR SCI	LITERATURE	6	41	77	0	124
		50.0%	37.3%	37.6%		37.9%
	SCIENCE	6	69	128	1	203
		50.0%	62.7%	62.4%		62.1%
	Missing	0	1	1	0	2
	TOTAL	12	110	205	1	327
		100.0%	100.0%	100.0%		

This second table is limited to males. The same thing here: no ring effect.

Let's try another.

Reading Playboy *Causes* Divorce

Dr. Pentunia Puffer today reported that the results of a five-year study show that the more copies of Playboy *that are sold, the higher the proportion of divorced people.*

*"It doesn't take a genius to understand this," Dr. Puffer said. "*Playboy *gives people an entirely false idea of what marriage is supposed to be like."*

Testifying before the North Dakota State Legislative Committee on Singleness, Dr. Puffer proposed a ban on the magazine and others like it. "Get this stuff off the newsstands and you will see a remarkable decline in divorce."

In subsequent testimony, former Playboy *Bunny, Belva Boom, protested that "lots of our readers are happily married."*

OPEN FILE: STATES

COMPARING MAPS:
    Variable 1: 20) %DIVORCED
    Variable 2: 46) PLAYBOY

%DIVORCED -- PERCENT OF THOSE 15 AND OVER WHO CURRENTLY ARE DIVORCED (CENSUS)

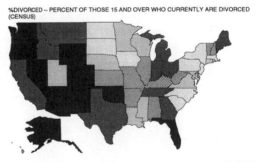

r = 0.412**

PLAYBOY -- PLAYBOY CIRCULATION PER 100,000 (ABC)

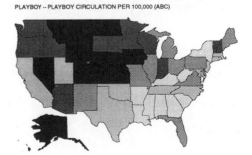

Just as Dr. Puffer claimed. There is a substantial and significant correlation between *Playboy* and divorce.

Exercise 15: Spuriousness

But, who reads *Playboy*, who gets divorced? Let's try this:

REGRESSION:
    Dependent Variable: 20) %DIVORCED
    Independent Variable: 46) PLAYBOY
    Independent Variable: 13) MALE HOMES

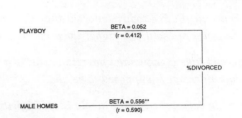

Where's the *Playboy* effect now? Men, especially men living in a household where there is no adult woman, read *Playboy* and lots of these same guys are divorced.

Another spurious relationship. And we know that because it disappeared when the real cause was held constant by means of regression. That is, a spurious correlation will not have a net effect (BETA will not be significant) when the real cause is included in the regression.

Your turn.

WORKSHEET

NAME:

COURSE:

DATE:

EXERCISE
15

REVIEW QUESTIONS

Based on the first part of this exercise, answer True or False to the following items:

There probably is a positive correlation between height and liking football.	T	F
People who don't wear rings are more likely to get in trouble with the police.	T	F
Both of the above are examples of a spurious relationship.	T	F
Playboy circulation is highly correlated with the percentage of male homes.	T	F
Spurious relationships exist when both variables share the same cause.	T	F

OPEN FILE: STATES

Newsflash:

Playboy Causes Alcohol Abuse

Where *Playboy* circulation is higher, alcohol consumption is higher too.

---

1. **COMPARING MAPS:**
   VARIABLE 1: 19) ALCOHOL
   VARIABLE 2: 46) PLAYBOY

   What is the value of r?   r = _____

   Is it negative or positive?   Negative   Positive

   Is it significant?   Yes   No

   Is the story supported or rejected?   Supported   Rejected

2. **REGRESSION:**
   DEPENDENT VARIABLE: 19) ALCOHOL
   INDEPENDENT VARIABLE: 46) PLAYBOY
   INDEPENDENT VARIABLE: 13) MALE HOMES

   What is the combined effect of these two independent variables?   _____

   What is the independent effect of PLAYBOY?   _____

   Is it negative or positive?   Negative   Positive

   Is it significant?   Yes   No

   What is the independent effect of MALE HOMES?   _____

   Is it negative or positive?   Negative   Positive

   Is it significant?   Yes   No

   Did the news story report a spurious relationship?   Spurious   Not Spurious

If the result is spurious, explain how it occurs (why *Playboy* and drinking are correlated).

_____

_____

_____

_____

_____

   OPEN FILE: GLOBAL

Newsflash:

New Research Reveals the Secret of Longer Life:
Take Drugs, Eat Meat, and Drink Lots of Alcohol

Medical experts are wearing sheepish grins today after learning that everything that was supposed to be bad for you in fact leads to a longer life.

You already have discovered these astounding medical facts in the previous exercise, so you can get right to work.

3. **COMPARING MAPS:**
      VARIABLE 1: 29) DRUG USE
      VARIABLE 2: 50) ECON DEVEL

      What is the value of r?   r = _____

      Is it negative or positive?   Negative   Positive

      Is it significant?   Yes   No

4. **COMPARING MAPS:**
      VARIABLE 1: 2) LIFE EXPEC
      VARIABLE 2: 50) ECON DEVEL

      What is the value of r?   r = _____

      Is it negative or positive?   Negative   Positive

      Is it significant?   Yes   No

      Do these results suggest that the news story is about spurious relationships? If so, why?

      _____

      _____

      _____

      _____

      _____

5. **REGRESSION:**
      DEPENDENT VARIABLE: 2) LIFE EXPEC
    INDEPENDENT VARIABLE: 29) DRUG USE
    INDEPENDENT VARIABLE: 50) ECON DEVEL

      What is the combined effect of these two independent variables?   _____

      What is the independent effect of DRUGS?   _____

Is it negative or positive?   Negative   Positive

Is it significant?   Yes   No

What is the independent effect of ECON DEVEL?   _____

Is it negative or positive?   Negative   Positive

Is it significant?   Yes   No

Did the news story report a spurious relationship?   Spurious   Not Spurious

6. **COMPARING MAPS:**
    VARIABLE 1: 25) MEAT CONS.
    VARIABLE 2: 50) ECON DEVEL

    What is the value of r?   r = _____

    Is it negative or positive?   Negative   Positive

    Is it significant?   Yes   No

    Do these results suggest that the news story is about spurious relationships? If so, why?

    _____

    _____

    _____

    _____

    _____

7. **REGRESSION:**
    DEPENDENT VARIABLE: 2) LIFE EXPEC
    INDEPENDENT VARIABLE: 25) MEAT CONS.
    INDEPENDENT VARIABLE: 50) ECON DEVEL

    What is the combined effect of these two independent variables?   _____

    What is the independent effect of MEAT CONS.?   _____

    Is it negative or positive?   Negative   Positive

Is it significant?   Yes   No

What is the independent effect of ECON DEVEL?   _____

Is it negative or positive?   Negative   Positive

Is it significant?   Yes   No

Did the news story report a spurious relationship?   Spurious   Not Spurious

8.   **COMPARING MAPS:**
     VARIABLE 1: 28) ALCOHOL
     VARIABLE 2: 50) ECON DEVEL

     What is the value of r?   r = _____

     Is it negative or positive?   Negative   Positive

     Is it significant?   Yes   No

     Do these results suggest that the news story is about spurious relationships? If so, why?

     _____

     _____

     _____

     _____

     _____

9.   **REGRESSION:**
     DEPENDENT VARIABLE: 2) LIFE EXPEC
     INDEPENDENT VARIABLE: 28) ALCOHOL
     INDEPENDENT VARIABLE: 50) ECON DEVEL

     What is the combined effect of these two independent variables?   _____

     What is the independent effect of ALCOHOL?   _____

     Is it negative or positive?   Negative   Positive

     Is it significant?   Yes   No

What is the independent effect of ECON DEVEL? _____

Is it negative or positive?   Negative   Positive

Is it significant?   Yes   No

Did the news story report a spurious relationship?   Spurious   Not Spurious

---

Newsflash:

Active People Live Longer

In nations where more people engage in sports, life expectancy is longer, experts say.

---

10. **COMPARING MAPS:**
    VARIABLE 1: 2) LIFE EXPEC
    VARIABLE 2: 27) DO SPORTS?

    What is the value of r?   r = _____

    Is it negative or positive?   Negative   Positive

    Is it significant?   Yes   No

    Is the story supported or rejected?   Supported   Rejected

11. **REGRESSION:**
    DEPENDENT VARIABLE: 2) LIFE EXPEC
    INDEPENDENT VARIABLE: 27) DO SPORTS?
    INDEPENDENT VARIABLE: 50) ECON DEVEL

    What is the combined effect of these two independent variables?   _____

    What is the independent effect of DO SPORTS?   _____

    Is it negative or positive?   Negative   Positive

    Is it significant?   Yes   No

What is the independent effect of ECON DEVEL?   _____

Is it negative or positive?   Negative   Positive

Is it significant?   Yes   No

Did the news story report a spurious relationship?   Spurious   Not Spurious

Appendix:
Variable Names and Sources

Note for users of the MicroCase Analysis System: These data files may be used with MicroCase. If you are moving variables from these files into other MicroCase files, or vice versa, you may need to reorder the cases. Also note that files that have been modified in MicroCase will not function properly in Student ExplorIt.

◆ DATA FILE: COLLEGE ◆

1) SEX
2) RINGS
3) PICKED UP?
4) LIT OR SCI

◆ DATA FILE: GLOBAL ◆

1) COUNTRY
2) LIFE EXPEC
3) $ GDP/CAP
4) HUMAN DEVL
5) GENDER POW
6) %FEM.PARL
7) INF MORTAL
8) MOM.MORT
9) %WITH AIDS
10) CIGARETTES
11) TV SETS
12) POPULATION
13) POP GROW
14) OVER 65
15) FERTILITY
16) CONTRACEP
17) CALORIES
18) AREA
19) DENSITY
20) %URBAN
21) LARGE FAML
22) ABORTION

23) ABORT LEGL
24) AB. UNWANT
25) MEAT CONS.
26) CARS/1000
27) DO SPORTS?
28) ALCOHOL
29) DRUG USE
30) VERY HAPPY
31) INTERESTED
32) SUICIDE NO
33) DIVORCE
34) CH.ATTEND
35) PRAY?
36) GOD EXISTS
37) %CHRISTIAN
38) %MUSLIM
39) GDP GROWTH
40) IMPORTS
41) $ RICH 10%
42) INEQUALITY
43) MULTI-CULT
44) C.CONFLICT

45) DEMOCRACY
46) EXPORTS
47) SINGLE MOM
48) WORK WARM
49) WED PASSE'
50) ECON DEVEL
51) SUICIDE
52) COASTLINE
53) ELECTRIC
54) ANTI-FORGN
55) RACISM
56) WORK PRIDE
57) ANTI-SEM.
58) ANTI-GAY
59) HOME LIFE?
60) HAPPY SEX?
61) CHORES?
62) UNIONIZED?
63) ECON REG.
64) HIGHER ED
65) EDUCATION
66) % IN AGR.

◆ DATA FILE: COUNTIES ◆

1) NAME
2) BUSH/GORE
3) % CATHOLIC
4) % JEWISH
5) %CH. MEMBR

6) POPULATION
7) % WHITE
8) % BLACK
9) % ASIAN
10) %P.ISLANDR

11) % HISPANIC
12) DIVERSITY
13) CRIME RATE
14) NOT MOVED
15) % A.INDIAN

◆ DATA FILE: STATES ◆

1) STATE NAME
2) POPULATION
3) WARM WINTR
4) % METROPOL
5) DENSITY
6) MED. AGE
7) MED.FAM$
8) % POOR
9) % STAYERS
10) POP GROW
11) % MOVERS
12) %NEWCOMERS
13) MALE HOMES
14) CH.MEMBERS
15) % NO RELIG
16) % JEWISH

17) BEER
18) WINE
19) ALCOHOL
20) %DIVORCED
21) ABORTIONS
22) SUICIDE
23) CRIME INDX
24) % FAT
25) SHRINKS
26) ASTROLOGER
27) HUNTERS
28) FLD&STREAM
29) COSMO
30) %SINGL MEN
31) %SINGL.FEM
32) %65 & OVER

33) DROP-OUTS
34) % COLLEGE
35) COL.DEGREE
36) % WHITE
37) %A.AMER
38) % HISPANIC
39) % ASIAN
40) % A.INDIAN
41) %P.ISLANDER
42) DIVERSITY
43) PICKUPS
44) CULTS
45) MARRY RATE
46) PLAYBOY
47) % BAPTIST
48) % CATHOLIC

◆ DATA FILE: SURVEY ◆

1) YEAR
2) REGION
3) SEX
4) RACE/ETHNI
5) WH/AF-AMER
6) AGE
7) OVR/UND 50
8) MARITAL
9) MARRYSINGL
10) FAMILY $
11) $ −50/+50K
12) EDUCATION
13) CH.ATTEND
14) REL CHOICE
15) ZODIAC
16) SEX ROLES
17) PARTY PREF
18) UNION MEMB
19) SUICIDE?
20) ABORT ANY?
21) UNFAITHFUL

22) HAPPY MAR?
23) SEX OFTEN?
24) #SEX PARTN
25) USE PC?
26) USE E-MAIL
27) CHAT ROOMS
28) READ PAPER
29) VERY HAPPY
30) WORK IF$$
31) GUN OWNER?
32) # KIDS
33) EMPLOYED?
34) MOM WORK?
35) WORK WARM
36) PRESCH.WRK
37) HOMEMAKER
38) FEM.PREZ
39) WORK/HOUSE
40) PRAYER?
41) TV TIME
42) CONCERTS

43) GO 2 MOVIE
44) READER?
45) GO 2 DOC?
46) GO 2 BARS
47) MOVERS
48) MARRY A-AM
49) MARRY HISP
50) MARRY ASIA
51) MARRY JEW
52) MARRY WHIT
53) BEEN DIVOR
54) JOB SATISF

◆ DATA FILE: TRENDS ◆

1) YEAR
2) POPULATION
3) IMMIGRAT'N
4) FERTILITY
5) LIFE EXPEC
6) MALE LIFEX
7) FEM LIFE X
8) FEM EXTRA
9) %<5
10) %65&OVER
11) % URBAN

12) % IN AGRIC
13) %HS
14) %COLLEGE
15) %UNEDUCATE
16) LAWYERS
17) DOCTORS
18) % FEM WORK
19) TELEPHONES
20) NEWSPAPERS
21) TELEVISION
22) TELEGRAMS

23) BOOKS
24) ELECTRICITY
25) PRICES
26) TB DEATHS
27) DIPHTHERIA
28) FLU&PNEUMO
29) CIRRHOSIS
30) TRAFFDEATH
31) SUICIDE

◆ DATA FILE: XCULT ◆

1) CASE NAME
2) WRITING
3) SLAVERY
4) STRATIFIED
5) STATE?
6) POLITICIAN
7) ENFORCERS
8) FIXITY
9) LOCAL POP.
10) ISOLATION

11) GATHER
12) WHEELS
13) WORK METAL
14) C.COMPLEX.
15) %FEM.SUBS
16) COUPLE BED
17) HOUSEWORK
18) WIFE DEFER
19) BEAT WIVES
20) OVER WIVES

21) F.INFERIOR
22) FEM.LIVES?
23) WARM:KIDS*
24) HIT KIDS
25) WAR
26) CIVIL WAR*
27) SOC.CONFL.
28) WARLIKE
29) CROSS-CUT?
30) REGION

SOURCES

COLLEGE

This data file is based on a survey of college freshmen enrolled at a university in the western part of the United States.

COUNTIES

The data in this file come from the most recent census, from CHURCH (see STATES), and from the 2000 election returns.

GLOBAL

The data in the GLOBAL file are from a variety of sources and are the most recent statistics available when the book went to press. The description of each variable includes one of the following abbreviations to indicate the source.

FITW: *Freedom in the World*, published periodically by Freedom House.

HDR: *Human Development Report*, published annually by the United Nations Development Program.

IP: *International Profile: Alcohol and Other Drugs*, published periodically by the Alcoholism and Drug Addiction Research Foundation, Toronto, Canada.

NBWR: *The New Book of World Rankings*, 3rd edition, Facts on File.

SAUS: *Statistical Abstract of the United States*, published annually by the U.S. Department of Commerce.

STARK: Coded and calculated by the author.

TWF: *The World Factbook*, published periodically by the Central Intelligence Agency.

TWW: *The World's Women*, published periodically by the United Nations.

UNSY: *United Nations Statistical Yearbook*.

WABF: *The World Almanac and Book of Facts*, published annually by World Almanac Books.

WCE: *World Christian Encyclopedia*, 2nd edition, Oxford University Press.

WVS: World Values Surveys.

HISTORY

The time series in this data file come from a variety of authoritative sources.

STATES

The data in the STATES file are from a variety of sources and are the most recent statistics available when the book went to press. The description of each variable includes one of the following abbreviations to indicate the source.

ABC: *Blue Book*, Audit Bureau of Circulation, published annually.

BADER: Data collected by Chris Bader.

CENSUS: Standard publications from the United States Bureau of the Census.

CHRON.: *Higher Education Almanac*, published annually by the Chronicle of Higher Education.

CHURCH: *Churches and Church Membership in the United States*, published every 10 years by the Glenmary Research Center, Atlanta.

HCSR: *Health Care State Rankings*, published annually by Morgan Quitno.

HIGHWAY: *Highway Statistics*, Federal Highway Administration, U.S. Department of Transportation.

KOSMIN: *The National Survey of Religious Identification*, Barry A. Kosmin, principal investigator, available from THE ARDA.COM.

KOSMIN AND LACHMAN: *One Nation Under God*, by Kosmin and Lachman, New York: Harmony Books.

MELTON: *Encyclopedia of American Religion*, by Gordon Melton, Gale, 1993.

SAUS: *Statistical Abstract of the United States*, published annually.

SR: *State Rankings*, published annually by Morgan Quitno.

U.S. FISH & WILDLIFE: Data provided by U.S. Fish and Wildlife Service.

SURVEY

Based on a merged file of the 1998 and 2000 General Social Surveys conducted by the National Opinion Research Center, University of Chicago. Principal investigators: James A. Davis and Tom W. Smith.

XCULT

This data file is based on the Standard Cross-Cultural Sample created by George Peter Murdock and Douglas R. White, *Ethnology*, 1971.